ANDREW J SIM

EVERYTHING YOUNG ATHLETES SHOULD KNOW

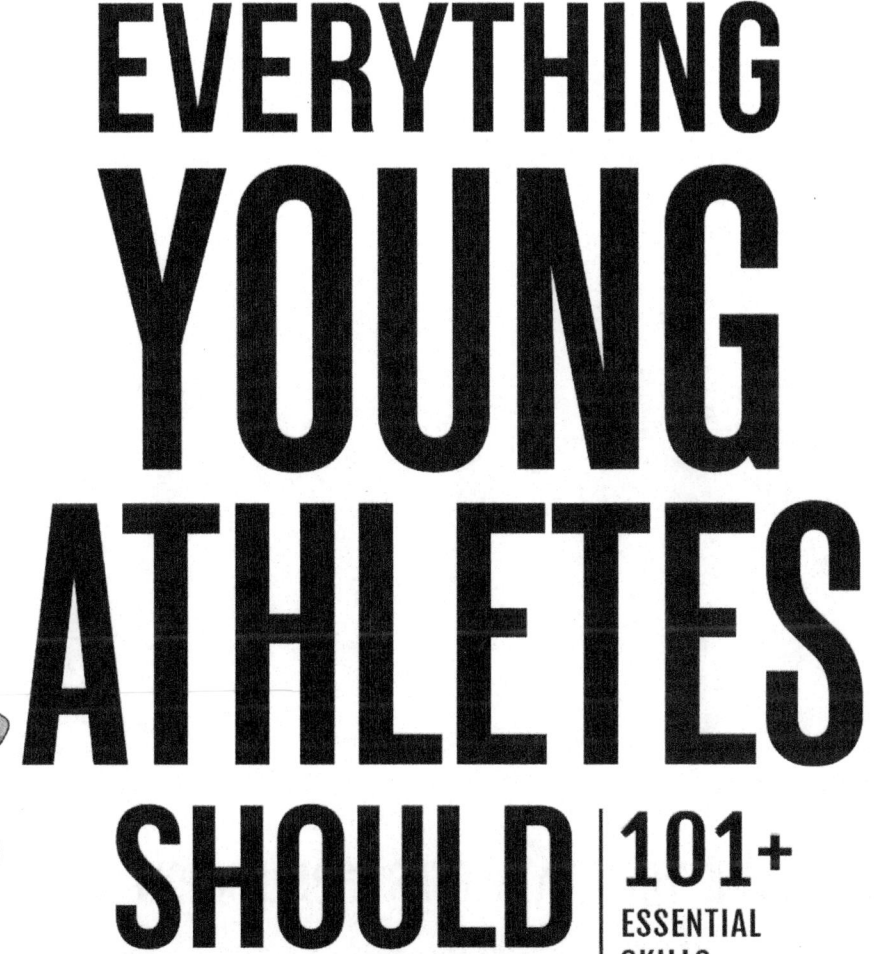

101+ ESSENTIAL SKILLS, STRATEGIES, & PRO TIPS FOR THRIVING IN SPORTS!

EVERYTHING YOUNG ATHLETES SHOULD KNOW

Copyright © 2025 by Andrew J Simpson

All rights reserved. No part of this publication may be reproduced, distributed, or transmitted in any form or by any means, including photocopying, recording, or other electronic or mechanical methods, without the prior written permission of the publisher, except in the case of brief quotations embodied in critical reviews and certain other noncommercial uses permitted by copyright law.

SCAN BELOW TO GET YOUR BONUSES!

- ✅ Pro Stretch and Recovery Video Series
- ✅ 8 Recruiting Resources to Save Time & Money
- ✅ Teenage Athlete Nutrition Journal Template
- ✅ What to Eat and When: Breakfast, Lunch, Pre-Workout, Post-Workout, and Dinner!
- ✅ All Accompanying PDF's and Resource Guides

Get The Entire Athlete Success Book Series!

Amazon Best Seller: 300+ 5-Star Reviews

The Unstoppable Athlete:
12 Keys to Unlock Your Full Potential
[The Only One Who Can Stop You, Is You]

The Youth Truth:

A Proven Playbook for Coaches and Parents to Develop Confident, Healthy, Wildly Successful Athletes without Adding Pressure or Pushing Them Away from Sports

Athlete! 7 Mindset Hacks to Dominate in Sports and Life:

Proven Strategies for Teen & College Athletes to Stop Overthinking, Get Out of Their Head, and Finally Master Their Mental Health and Mindset

TABLE OF CONTENTS

INTRODUCTION
EVERYTHING YOUNG ATHLETES SHOULD KNOW 1

THE FIRST ESSENTIAL AREA OF MASTERY
MINDSET, MOTIVATION, & MENTAL TOUGHNESS 5

1. Pre-Game Self Talk to Get in the Zone 6
2. Self Talk to Push Past Pain and Discomfort 7
3. Self Talk to Overcome Mistakes 9
4. Self Talk After a "Bad" Game 10
5. How to Turn Pressure into Power 12
6. Overcoming Perfectionism 13
7. Managing Your Emotions 15
8. Advanced Visualization Technique 16
9. Overcoming the Fear of Failing 18
10. Avoid Burnout and Keep Your Passion High 19
11. How to Stay Motivated 21
12. Creating Your Pre-Game Routines 22
13. How to Stay Focused 24
14. How to Increase Confidence 25
15. How to Handle Success Like a Champion 26
16. Energy Management for Less Stress and Better Performance, Part 1 28
17. Energy Management for Less Stress and Better Performance, Part 2: Mastering Transitions 29
18. Energy Management for Less Stress and Better Performance, Part 3: Transitioning From Season to Season 30
19. Staying Present: The Power of WIN 31

THE SECOND ESSENTIAL AREA OF MASTERY
DREAMING BIG AND ACHIEVING IMPOSSIBLE GOALS 35

20. 4 Critical Errors in Goal-Setting That Can Cost You 36
21. The Power of Goal Setting: Key Benefits Explained, Part 1 37
22. The Power of Goal Setting: Key Benefits Explained, Part 2 38
23. The Art of Successful Goal Setting, Part 1: Defining Your "Becoming" Goals... 39
24. The Art of Successful Goal Setting, Part 2: Creating Your BHAG..... 41
25. The Art of Successful Goal Setting, Part 3: Developing a Clear Plan of Action... 43
26. Crafting Short-Term, Tiered Goals... 44
27. How to Craft Bottom Tier, "Survive" Goals 45
28. How to Craft Mid Tier, "Succeed" Goals 47
29. How to Craft Top Tier, "Transform" Goals 48

THE THIRD ESSENTIAL AREA OF MASTERY
PHYSICAL SKILLS, STRENGTH, SPEED, AND STAMINA: HOW TO TRAIN HARD, SMART, & MAXIMIZE PHYSICAL ATHLETICISM FOR ANY SPORT 51

30. Overview: Performance Training and Skill Development 52
31. Hiring a Performance Coach vs. Doing it on Your Own 52
32. Things You Should Know Before You Invest in a Personal Trainer... 54
33. How to Build Serious Strength 55
34. Becoming Powerful and Explosive... 57
35. Training for Looks Vs. Performance 58
36. The Best Kept Secrets for Getting Faster.. 59
37. 7 Advanced Tips for Improving Your Speed... 60
38. Improving Endurance and Stamina 62
39. Improving Rhythm, Balance, and Coordination 64
40. Sport Specific Training.. 65
41. From Talent to Mastery: Skill Development Specific to Your Sport... 67
42. Planning, Accountability, and Intensity 69

THE FOURTH ESSENTIAL AREA OF MASTERY
FUELING LIKE A GOLD MEDALIST: NUTRITION AND HYDRATION DOS AND DON'TS 71

43. Overview: Nutrition and Fueling for Performance 72
44. Nutrition and The Law of the Path 73
45. Don't Be Fooled! Reading Nutrition Labels & Ingredient Lists 73
46. Hydration Essentials 76
47. The Truth About Sports Drinks | By: Sarah Stack 78
48. Quick Tips and Swaps to Fuel Performance 79

THE FIFTH ESSENTIAL AREA OF MASTERY
RECOVERY, SLEEP, & INJURY PREVENTION: THE UNSEEN HABITS OF THE BEST ATHLETES ON THE PLANET 81

49. Recovery and Sleep: Habits of the Best Athletes on the Planet 82
50. The Power of Sleep: How Missing Rest Impacts Your Growth 82
51. Building Healthy Sleep Habits, Part 1 84
52. Building Healthy Sleep Habits, Part 2 85
53. Active Recovery Vs. Time Off 86
54. How to Increase Flexibility, Reduce Soreness, & Recover Faster with Foam Rolling 88
55. Sport Specific Stretches 89
56. The Power of Breathing 92

THE SIXTH ESSENTIAL AREA OF MASTERY
SELF LEADERSHIP, LEADING OTHERS, & STRENGTHENING RELATIONSHIPS 95

57. The Most Important Thing About Sports That No One Teaches You 96
58. Fostering Team Cohesion: The Role You Play in Creating Unity ... 96
59. The #1 Threat to Team Harmony—and How You Can Stop It 97
60. How to Win the Trust and Respect of Your Teammates 99
61. Improve Your Relationship With Coaches and Older Teammates 101
62. How to Be a Leader to Your Teammates Who Are Peers 102
63. How to Lead Your Younger, Less Experienced Teammates 103
64. How to Have "Difficult" Conversations and Confront People Without Making Them Feel *Less* Than You 105

65. What To Do When Teammates Don't Care As Much As You Do ... 106
66. What To Do If You Are Feeling Pressure From Parents 108

THE SEVENTH ESSENTIAL AREA OF MASTERY
YOUR CHARACTER COUNTS FOR DOUBLE POINTS 111

67. Humility 112
68. GRIT 113
69. Discipline 114
70. Responsibility and Taking Ownership 116
71. Long-Range Patience, Part 1 117
72. Long-Range Patience, Part 2: The Bamboo Tree 118
73. Integrity 120
74. Enthusiasm 121
75. Poise 122
76. Don't Cut Corners, Do the Work and Do it Well 123
77. Self Control 125
78. Self Worth 126
79. Competitive Spirit 128
80. Aggressiveness 129

THE EIGHTH ESSENTIAL AREA OF MASTERY
WINNING THE RECRUITING GAME + EVERYTHING YOU SHOULD KNOW ABOUT PLAYING COLLEGE SPORTS 131

81. Overview: Recruiting and the College Sports Landscape 132
82. 7 Costly Mistakes Parents and Coaches Make During the Recruiting Process 133
83. Define Your Vision & Commit to the Process 134
84. Know the Landscape 136
85. The Power of Academics 138
86. Research and Discover Your Best Fit 140
87. Build Your Brand, Market Yourself, and Be Seen 142
88. Weigh Your Options and Select the Best Fit 145
89. College Sports: New Level, New Devil, New Skills Required 146
90. Behind the Recruiting Pitch: The Coach You Meet vs. The Coach You Get 148
91. Pause: Is Playing College Sports REALLY What You Want? ... 149

THE NINTH ESSENTIAL AREA OF MASTERY
EMPOWERING FEMALE ATHLETES: OPTIMIZING PERFORMANCE WITHOUT SACRIFICING HEALTH..................153

- **92.** 6 Unique Needs for Female Athletes.................154
- **93.** Performance Training for the Female Athlete 155
- **94.** 3 Steps to Prevent ACL Injuries, Part 1 156
- **95.** 3 Steps to Prevent ACL Injuries, Part 2 161
- **96.** Nutrition for the Female Athlete, Part 1.................163
- **97.** Nutrition for the Female Athlete, Part 2.................166

THE TENTH ESSENTIAL AREA OF MASTERY
INSPIRING GREATNESS: 10 LITTLE KNOWN TIPS FOR ATHLETES WITH TRANSFORMATIONAL POWER..................169

- **98.** Luck vs. Hard work.................170
- **99.** Keep Going Until You Get it Right.................170
- **100.** Practice Like It's Gametime.................171
- **101.** It's You vs. You.................172
- **102.** Willpower Doesn't Work.................173
- **103.** Don't Just Go Through The Motions.................174
- **104.** Sports are a Gift, not an Entitlement.................174
- **105.** Vulnerability is Power.................175
- **106.** The Secret to Never Ending Motivation.................176
- **107.** Choose Fun, Play the Long Game.................177

CONCLUSION.................179

INTRODUCTION

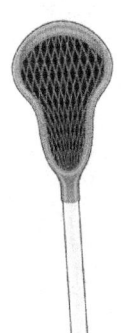

EVERYTHING YOUNG ATHLETES SHOULD KNOW

EVERYTHING YOUNG ATHLETES SHOULD KNOW

Hey, athlete! Coach Andrew here. I am so excited for you to experience the life changing benefits from this book.

As a performance coach, I've had the privilege of helping thousands of athletes overcome mental and physical barriers, unlocking their true potential as both athletes and leaders.

Part of the challenge for athletes like you is that there are so, so many things athletes need to know and master if they are going to be successful. The number of things that are on your mind and on your plate can be overwhelming!

Fortunately, you now have everything you need in one place. The 106 chapters ahead are packed with the key lessons and strategies for success. And don't worry—each chapter is only 1-2 pages long!

There are 10 Essential Areas of Mastery that you must focus on. These are crucial for reaching your biggest goals without burning out or losing momentum.

Knowing these areas is just the beginning—applying them consistently will be transformational. You may already be excelling in some, which is awesome—keep it up!

For the areas that are new to you or need more consistency, I recommend doubling down on your effort. You put in too much hard work and passion to overlook key opportunities for improvement! Now, let's go through an overview of each area you will be mastering throughout this book:

The first essential area of mastery for young athletes is called "Mindset, Motivation, and Mental Toughness." Most athletes are told to "just get out of your head," or to "stay focused," or to "be more motivated." The truth is that those are skills you need to learn and develop.

EVERYTHING YOUNG ATHLETES SHOULD KNOW

The second essential area of mastery is "Dreaming Big and Achieving Impossible Goals." Can you *see* the future greatness that is in store for you? In section two, I will help you *see* it, *plan* for it, and *achieve* it.

The third essential area of mastery is "Physical Skills, Strength, Speed, and Stamina: How to Train Hard, Train Smart, and Maximize Physical Athleticism for Any Sport." Many athletes are leaving performance on the table by not addressing certain areas of athleticism properly. Not after reading this section!

The fourth essential area of mastery is "Fueling Like a Gold Medalist: Nutrition and Hydration Dos and Don'ts." Many athletes put minor focus on this major area of sports. You'll learn what to eat, when to eat it, and how much to eat in this section.

The fifth essential area of mastery is "Recovery, Sleep, and Injury Prevention: The Unseen Habits of the Best Athletes on the Planet." Training hard without a focus on recovery is like watering a plant and then putting it in a dark room with no sunlight. Your growth will be stunted without proper rest!

The sixth essential area of mastery is "Self-Leadership, Leading Others, and Strengthening Relationships." People are the point, both in sports and in life. Like sleep, relationship management is a major impact area that gets minor focus and attention.

The seventh essential area of mastery is "Your Character Counts for Double Points." At the end of the day, who you *become* is more important than what you *accomplish*. If you want to achieve more, you must first *become* more!

The eighth essential area of mastery is "Winning the Recruiting Game + Everything You Should Know About Playing College Sports." The best

EVERYTHING YOUNG ATHLETES SHOULD KNOW

time to learn something is *before* you need to. No matter your age or stage, this section will help you achieve your dreams without wasting unnecessary time, energy, or money.

The ninth essential area of mastery is specifically for young female athletes and is called "Empowering Female Athletes: Optimizing Performance without Sacrificing Health." Based on the limited amount of quality information dedicated to the uniqueness of the female athlete, this area felt important to include. If you are a young male athlete, you can skip this one or be a leader; take pictures of the chapters and send them to your sister or female friends!

The tenth essential area of mastery for young athletes is "Inspiring Greatness: 10 Little Known Tips for Athletes with Transformational Power." This section is packed with rare, inspiring quotes and tips from coaches and professional athletes.

Now, let's jump into our first tip, part of the "Mindset, Motivation, and Mental Toughness" area of mastery.

THE FIRST
ESSENTIAL AREA OF MASTERY

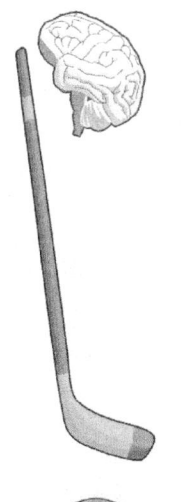

MINDSET, MOTIVATION, & MENTAL TOUGHNESS

EVERYTHING YOUNG ATHLETES SHOULD KNOW

1. Pre-Game Self Talk to Get in the Zone

Your words, spoken and unspoken, have weight. It is said that, "Those who fail to prepare, prepare to fail."

Every athlete must know what to say to themselves in order to get into the zone of excellence.

If you do not choose what to say to yourself before a game, you will default to your natural thoughts.

But what are your natural thoughts?

Are you naturally positive toward yourself? Do you mentally encourage yourself often?

Probably not.

Many athletes are naturally critical and doubt their own abilities.

You may default to phrases like:

"I hope I don't mess up."

"I really hope the coach plays me today."

"That guy on the other team is so fast, I don't know how I will be able to keep up."

Compare that to the following self talk:

"I am more prepared than I have ever been."

"I am confident. I am courageous."

"I will lead. I will leave it ALL on the field today."

Write your new, encouraging pre-game self talk in the space below:

_____
_____
_____
_____
_____
_____
_____
_____
_____

2. Self Talk to Push Past Pain and Discomfort

"Where there is no pain, there is no gain." This is not entirely true, because some types of pain are unhelpful, unnatural, and unnecessary.

The pain of being verbally abused by a coach, for example, is NOT to be tolerated.

The sharp pain of shin splints or an injured shoulder should NOT be ignored. You need to address that with a doctor!

The type of pain I am referring to, that EVERY young athlete should know about and push past, is the physical discomfort that comes from pushing yourself in the weight room, during physical conditioning, and throughout intense skill development sessions.

EVERYTHING YOUNG ATHLETES SHOULD KNOW

A cross country runner that I coach was really struggling when he got to mile 3 of his 5 mile races.

"When I get to mile 3 and it starts to hurt, I begin rehearsing how bad it hurts in my mind and how I want to give up," he courageously shared with me.

We created a new self-talk routine specifically for times of pain or discomfort. It is as follows:

"EVERY step, EVERY rep, I am getting STRONGER and STRONGER."

He also added the following self-talk: "I CAN AND I WILL!"

He now repeats those phrases with passion during his races and is able to push through discomfort that used to stop him in his tracks.

Write your new self talk routine for discomfort in the space below:

_____

_____

_____

_____

_____

_____

_____

_____

_____

3. Self Talk to Overcome Mistakes

Every athlete needs a customized technique that is unique to you for moments when you lose focus, get frustrated, or shift into an unhelpful frame of mind. The Mindset Reset Tool is a tool to help you avoid focusing on the things you cannot change and instead get focused on what is in front of you, the things you *can* change.

Part 1: Choose Your Word or Phrase

FOCUS – POWERFUL – OVERCOME – NEXT – ONWARD – I'VE GOT THIS – CONFIDENT – DOMINATE – NEXT PLAY

MY WORD/PHRASE: _____

These are examples of words that other athletes have chosen. The word itself is less important than what it MEANS to you. The word you choose should have power and meaning for YOU.

Part 2: Choose a Strong Hand Signal

CLAP ONCE – CLAP TWICE – SNAP YOUR FINGERS – SLAP YOUR LEG – HAND TO FIST – OPEN AND CLOSE HAND – TAP YOUR HEAD – SLAP BOTH LEGS

MY HAND SIGNAL: _____

Again, the most important part of this is that you choose a hand signal that matches your RESET WORD. Pick a hand signal that makes you feel powerful, strong, like you can and will OVERCOME. Be unstoppable.

Part 3: Link the two together with a DEEP BREATH

Now, if you are like me, you are going to get excited about this, try it a few times, and then stop doing it.

> "Successful people do repeatedly what unsuccessful people do occasionally."

Make a commitment to yourself right now that you will establish your reset tool today and use it every day.

Why? Because it works. It has worked for every single athlete that I have ever worked with.

Make sure to grab the bonuses that come with the book (www.andrewjsimpson.com/everything-bonus), as I have included a video teaching where I help you create your Mindset Reset Tool..

4. Self Talk After a "Bad" Game

What do you tell yourself after a bad game?

Again, if you do not pre-plan the positive things that you are going to say to yourself, you may end up with negative self-talk.

"See, I knew this would happen. I always mess up."

"I'm not worthy."

"I might as well give up on my dream."

"We are never going to win the conference."

"That was a 'bad' game."

I put quotes around "bad" because games are not good nor bad. They are neutral.

How you look at the game determines whether or not you get better or bitter afterwards.

MINDSET, MOTIVATION, & MENTAL TOUGHNESS

Is winning actually better than losing? Do you learn more from winning or losing? Can you learn from both?

Of course you can.

An example of post-game self talk after a tough loss or poor performance could be as follows:

"Sometimes I win, sometimes I learn. I will get better from this."

"24 hours. Then I will figure out what I can do to improve."

"Next."

"This doesn't change anything. I am still on track for my goals."

Write your new self talk routine after a "bad game" in the space below:

_____

_____

_____

_____

_____

_____

_____

_____

_____

EVERYTHING YOUNG ATHLETES SHOULD KNOW

5. How to Turn Pressure into Power

Before I teach you how to turn pressure into power, which is an incredible skill to have, I want to be real with you…

The pressure *will* rise as you get more and more serious about your sport.

You must decide right now that you will have the courage to be open, honest, and vulnerable with others throughout your athletic journey. You likely have at least one person, maybe it's a parent, with whom you can be completely transparent about how you are feeling. If you cannot think of a person with whom you can be transparent, you should ask a friend or loved one to help you find a therapist, counselor, or mindset coach.

Athletes who fail to open up about the honest pressures they are feeling end up anxious, depressed, and sometimes in a very dark place.

Don't let that be you. Decide now that as you begin to feel the pressures of higher and higher level sports, you will actively open up about it with those you trust most.

Ok, back to turning pressure into power. Where does pressure come from? Is it real? Is it made up in your mind? Can you touch it? See it?

You say that your parents *put* pressure on you. You say that your coach *adds* pressure to you. But what *is* pressure? Is it something that has the power to crush you? Or, is it something that has the power to make *diamonds*?

First, to deal with pressure you must first acknowledge that it is not actually a real thing. Can you show me what pressure looks like? Of course not. It's a made up thing in your mind.

Second, you will need to change the way you *think* about what you are feeling.

If you are feeling a "weight" on your shoulders, could that actually be a good thing? Without that weight, you may not work as hard!

Usually when an athlete feels pressure, they are overthinking about the future in a negative way.

The 3 steps to overcome pressure are to:

1. Determine your own goals and your own time frame to achieve them.
2. Thank other people for encouraging you to accomplish certain goals, but do not accept them as pressure. Go back to YOUR goals and stay focused on them.
3. When someone tries to hand you pressure-packed expectations, simply refuse the pressure. If someone hands you a gift, and you do not accept it, to whom does the gift belong? **Hint**: Not you! You do not have to accept the "gift" of pressure.

Lastly, if the pressure has become too great for you to bear and you are feeling overwhelming emotional pain, I encourage you to pick up a phone and dial 988. This is extreme courage in action.

6. Overcoming Perfectionism

Perfectionists almost never end up reaching their full potential because they burn themselves out long before they ever get close to that potential.

The pursuit of perfection is a great thing, as long as you realize and accept that you will never reach it.

The entire goal of pursuing perfection is to make more progress than you would have otherwise.

EVERYTHING YOUNG ATHLETES SHOULD KNOW

Here is how to overcome the negative effects of perfectionism:

1. Create a habit of measuring your progress BACKWARDS against where you used to be, not against your bigger and better future goals. Writing exercises:
    i. Once a week, write down ALL of your wins, your positives, and the ways you improved in the last week.
    ii. At the end of a season, reflect back on the entire season and do the same thing.
    iii. Once a year, write down all the ways you are better or different than you were this time last year.
    iv. Every 5 years, do the same thing.

2. Set clear goals.

    Broad goals like "get faster" or "score a lot of goals" will leave you dissatisfied and frustrated because they are not specific enough.

    Setting big, clear goals will set you up for success not only because they will motivate you, but because of the sense of encouragement you will feel as you make tangible progress toward those goals. Not to mention when you reach them! That sense of accomplishment will fuel you to set, and reach, even bigger goals in the future.

Satisfaction as an athlete is a good thing; it encourages you and puts you in a positive state of mind so you actually perform better! Refuse to fall into the "never be satisfied" trap.

There is a go-to exercise I teach athletes how to do that will really help with replacing your unhealthy perfectionism with a healthy dose of feeling proud and accomplished. I wrote about that extensively in my book, *Athlete! I'm Talking To You.*

7. Managing Your Emotions

Tony Dungy, former head coach of the Indianapolis Colts, found that most athletes have trouble controlling their emotions. His solution was to teach his players to ACT MEDIUM. This is a concept he used to produce a Super Bowl winning team.

What goes up must come down.

When something goes down, it takes a lot of energy to get back up.

Acting medium is the best way to maintain consistent, peak performance. If you struggle with having consistency in your performance, it's probably due to the fact that you have inconsistent emotions.

ACTING MEDIUM

When things go poorly, the best athletes stay calm, cool, and collected. They do not let their emotions get overly *high* when things go well, nor do they let themselves get too *low* when things are not going well.

How do I handle my emotions when things do not go as planned? Do I get upset easily? Do I get frustrated too quickly? Write about your current emotional management below:

_____

_____

_____

_____

How do I want to act when things do not go as planned? With a smile and a deep breath? By high fiving my teammates and saying *"Forget about that, we've got this."* Write about your ideal emotions when things are not going your way.

_____

_____

_____

_____

_____

In the moment when you feel yourself starting to lose control of your emotions, take a deep breath and repeat these words to yourself: "Act Medium."

8. Advanced Visualization Technique

You cannot be what you cannot see. If you cannot see yourself being successful, you won't be successful. Vision is the front door into your best performance.

The problem is that most athletes have learned a watered down version of visualization and they don't fully believe in it. If that's you, this will change the game. **Advanced visualization is when you get more of your senses involved and you activate your physiology in the process!**

PRE-WORK:

Decide how you are going to celebrate after success. See it. Feel it. Are you going to throw your arms up in a victory pose? Are you going to run to your teammate and chest bump them? Are you going to yell?

MINDSET, MOTIVATION, & MENTAL TOUGHNESS

Step 1: Decide *what* you are going to visualize. Is it an offensive play? Defensive? A game winning shot? A routine at bat? The way you are going to respond to getting beat by an offensive player?

Step 2: Stand up (unless you are seated in your sport, i.e. a chess player) and move like you are ready to perform. Shift your weight side to side, move your body, and get yourself into the feelings of a live game.

Step 3: See everything you would normally see. The fans, the stadium/atmosphere, the scoreboard, the painted lines, the basket, etc. See it all.

Step 4: Hear everything you would normally hear. The fans, coach yelling (but then, silence that). Hear your teammates cheering for you. Hear the wind blowing. Hear the bat clank against your cleats.

Step 5: Go through the event, full speed. If you are a swimmer, you better be moving those arms whether you are in the pool or not. If you are a softball player, you better be in your full blown hitting stance and execute the motion at full speed.

Step 6: Celebrate. Yes, literally celebrate as if you just accomplished the goal.

Step 7: Do it again for a new area of sports that you want to be successful in!

Visualization works, but advanced visualization works better.

If visualization hasn't worked in the past, it is likely because you didn't know the right way to do it, and didn't stick with it long enough.

9. Overcoming the Fear of Failing

What has to happen in order for you to feel like you have failed?

Are you making it too easy for yourself to feel like a failure?

Take, for example, my old definition of failure:

> "Andrew, if you mess up, fall short of perfection, or don't perform at the highest level you've ever performed in the game today, *you are a failure.*"

Whoa! It's no wonder why I used to play scared, which *always* led to performing less than my best!

A coach taught me that I had the power to create my own definition of failure, and ultimately, success.

He said to me, "Andrew, since feeling like a failure is not helping your performance, I suggest you create a definition of failure that makes it hard for you to experience."

Andrew's New Definition of Failure: I have to completely give up on something just because it got hard, THEN I will allow myself to feel the intense feelings of failure.

I really like my new definition because I do not have to fear that happening often, and when it does, it really motivates me to never feel it again!

The way you define failure and success will determine a lot about your mental performance, which in turn leads to your physical performance.

MINDSET, MOTIVATION, & MENTAL TOUGHNESS

Take some time below to reflect on your old definition of failure, then write your new definition!

Write Your Old Definition of Failure in the space below:

_____
_____
_____
_____

Write Your New Definition of Failure in the space below:

_____
_____
_____
_____

10. Avoid Burnout and Keep Your Passion High

> *"Passion is a huge prerequisite to winning. It makes you willing to jump through hoops, go through all the ups and downs and everything in between to reach your goal."*
>
> - KERRI WALSH JENNINGS, TEAM USA OLYMPIC BEACH VOLLEYBALL PLAYER

Why are some elite, professional, and Olympic-level athletes able to get to the top of their game and stay there for longer than others?

Does the money keep them passionate?

EVERYTHING YOUNG ATHLETES SHOULD KNOW

Probably not. Money cannot make you a mentally tough, healthy, happy, and high-performing athlete.

3 Rules to Keep Your Passion High

Rule #1: Don't lose it to begin with.

Burnout occurs one practice, one game, one day, one week, one month, one season, one year at a time. Pay attention to when you are beginning to experience a lack of joy in your sport, and then consider taking action on rule #2.

Rule #2: Take regular time off from your sport, or be forced to take time off later.

Many overuse injuries and mental breakdowns could have been prevented had the athlete had the discipline and foresight to take time off, rest, and recover, both mentally and physically.

Rule #3: Avoid The 5 Passion Killers:

1. Having no hobbies and no life outside of your sport.
2. Getting bored with the basics and failing to master your craft. It has been confirmed through research that *passion comes after mastery.*
3. Failing to recognize your progress, wins, and growth.
4. Not creating meaningful connections with your coach & teammates.
5. Not having goals or a compelling vision for the future.

Difficult circumstances do not lead to burnout or loss of passion. It's a combination of the 5 passion killers.

One more important piece of advice for you– there is no greater detriment to your passion, energy, and joy than saying *yes* to every opportunity that comes your way. Saying yes to every club team that approaches you, for example, will eventually cost you your passion.

Keeping the "first things first" is the best way to avoid burnout and keep your passion high.

What are these "first things?"

It's your family, friends, health, and academics. You already knew that, but I wanted to remind you!

11. How to Stay Motivated

Have you ever been really motivated and then lost that motivation?

Think about a time when you were super motivated. What caused you to be so motivated?

It's likely that you were motivated to get something that you wanted in the future. The more you thought about the goal, result, or outcome, the more motivated you became!

Perhaps you were motivated to get recognition from your coach, earn a physical trophy or accolade, or achieve the status of being the best on the team/top scorer/an all-conference player.

Maybe you were motivated because a college coach was coming to watch you.

Or, you may have been motivated by fear. The fear of not making a team, the fear of showing up to tryouts and teammates thinking you didn't work hard over the summer, or the fear that you won't be accepted or loved by parents if you don't perform well.

EVERYTHING YOUNG ATHLETES SHOULD KNOW

Fear is a tremendous short term motivator but often also a motivator that leads to long-term burnout.

The key to staying motivated is to:

1. **Create Alignment.** Make sure you are aligned with who you really are and what you really want. People who are chasing things they don't truly want eventually lose motivation. And people who are trying to be someone they are not *always* lose motivation.
2. **Act the way you want to feel first, and eventually, you will feel the way you acted.** Motivation is the result of action, not the other way around. When you are stagnant or sluggish, you are simply more motivated to stay still than you are to move. Start moving - then you will feel more motivated!
3. **Hang around with motivated people.** This can actually be a good motivator in and of itself. Motivated people like to hang around motivated people. If you want to be around those types of people more often (who doesn't?) then *be* that person first!

12. Creating Your Pre-Game Routines

Have you ever seen an athlete who bounces around with excitement and enthusiasm before competitions? An example of this kind of athlete is Noah Lyles, 2024 Olympic Gold Medalist in the 100 meter dash.

What about an athlete who sits quietly before games, not moving much, listening to music? An example of this kind of athlete is Stephen Nedoroscik, 2024 Olympic Pommel Horse Medalist who came through clutch for team USA in the all around final. Did you watch that? It was crazy!

Some athletes perform best when they get hyped up before games, while some athletes play best when they are more calm.

MINDSET, MOTIVATION, & MENTAL TOUGHNESS

Which is better, being pumped up and energetic before games OR being quiet, laid back, and chill?

NEITHER! All that matters is that you know what *your* sweet spot is and you aim to get there *consistently*.

The U-curve, illustrated in the graphic below, will help you identify your area of best performance.

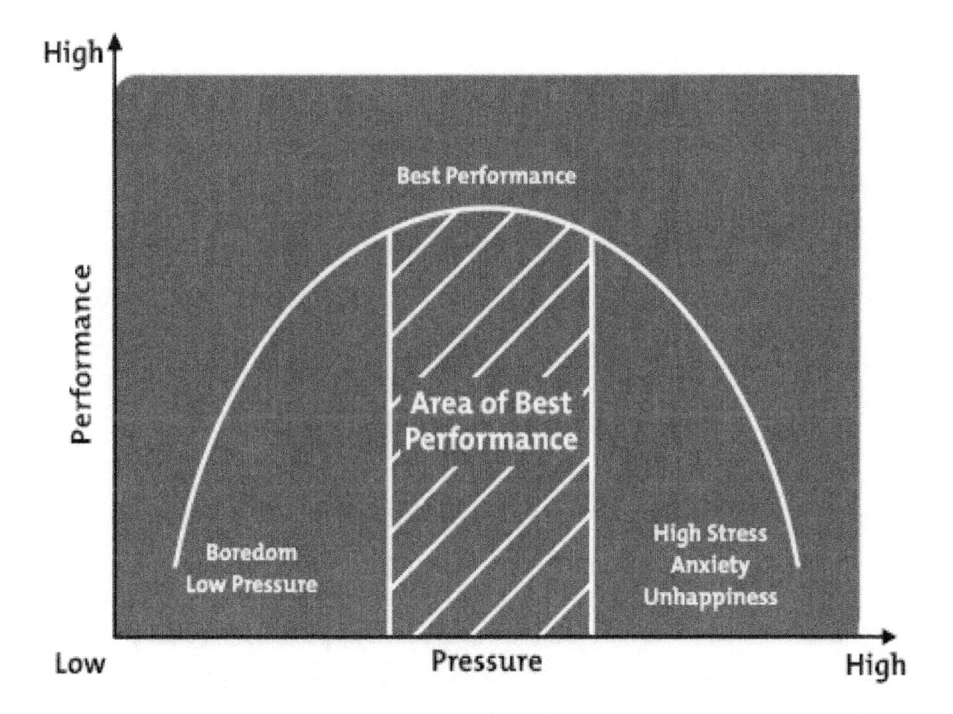

Two key questions:

1. Do you perform best when you are super pumped up and excited, super chill and relaxed, or somewhere in between?
2. What do you need to do before games to get there?

EVERYTHING YOUNG ATHLETES SHOULD KNOW

13. How to Stay Focused

Have your coaches or parents ever called you out for not being focused enough?

Mine have.

What's the opposite of focus?

Distracted.

What distracts us?

Everything.

The 3 secrets to focusing with laser-like intensity are to:

1. Eliminate all distractions

The more often an athlete scrolls social media or jumps from video to video on different media platforms, the worse their ability to stay focused is.

Think about how quickly you scroll from one post to the next, or jump from one video to the next. Those actions are creating a habit of distraction for you. Each time you scroll from one clip to the next, you are teaching your brain to be more distracted.

Eliminate as many social media or video apps from your phone as possible, and watch your focus SOAR! At minimum, reduce screen time. This will help as well.

2. Get connected to a huge motivating goal

We are going to talk about goals *a lot* in this book. Nothing creates focus like a huge goal.

Think about playing darts, or basketball. There is no way to be successful unless you are locked in on the target.

3. Use self-talk that promotes FOCUS!

Repeat phrases like "Lock in, Andrew!" or, "Focus, Andrew!" in your mind - or out loud! If you find yourself getting distracted by caring too much about what others are thinking about you, use self-talk to combat it.

Any one of those three keys above will help you stay focused. Now, don't just stand there, go apply them!

14. How to Increase Confidence

Cory is a 16-year-old lacrosse player who is undersized and lacking confidence.

He wanted to get stronger, but he lacked confidence in his abilities in the weight room because he had never done it before. He procrastinated for 3 months before going to the gym with a personal trainer his parents had arranged. *Avoidance* is a great short-term strategy to feel comfortable, but a long-term plan to be miserable!

Finally, he realized that things would never change unless *he changed*.

Within 12 weeks, he put on roughly six pounds of muscle and people started noticing. His confidence and belief in himself went through the roof. He started driving to the goal more, first in practice, then in games. Before long, he started scoring goals. And then, more goals.

He began engaging in conversations with his coaches more. He started putting himself out there in social situations.

> You will gain confidence once you begin *doing* the very thing that you have been procrastinating about or have been scared to do. Repetition lead to confidence.

Are you lacking confidence in your ability to dribble a basketball? The key to confidence is to practice dribbling, especially on days you don't feel like it, until you start to feel confident.

Not confident in driving to the goal? Start doing it at practice! Ignore people who discourage you from getting reps in and just start doing it.

Not confident in throwing a pass as you are moving to your left? Work at it constantly.

You generate confidence by doing confidence-generating things day, after day, after day. When you practice purposefully and improve in something, your confidence muscles contract and get bigger.

Confident people were not born confident. They learned it and then generated it. Remember this: confident people are simply willing to *do* the things that others are not willing to do.

15. How to Handle Success Like a Champion

Most athletes only think about how to *become* successful. Few ever learn how to *continue to be successful.* The only way you will become successful and sustain success is if you learn how to handle success like a champion.

Have you ever achieved success in something and then felt like you didn't deserve it? Have you ever reached a big goal and then started to become complacent and not work as hard? Have you ever achieved something in sports, only to then be criticized, made fun of, told "you got lucky," or ridiculed by a friend?

Being successful is *not* easy. Even if you become successful one time, it does not mean you are guaranteed to always be successful.

MINDSET, MOTIVATION, & MENTAL TOUGHNESS

This is because there is a right way and a wrong way to handle success. The truth is that only a few athletes handle success like a champion. But you can be one of them!

Here is how to handle success like a champion:

1. Be Prepared

Once you are successful, be prepared for a wide variety of feedback. "Good job. I wish I was you." This could lead to you feeling guilty that your friend didn't achieve as much, leading you to start subconsciously giving less effort because you don't want them to feel bad again.

2. Be Humble, Stay Hungry

A great response to success is this: "I feel really great about this accomplishment. I am proud of what I've done so far. I am going to use this to fuel me to continue pushing and getting better. I have not arrived yet; I am a work in progress. This is only the beginning."

3. Don't Let People Put You on a Pedestal

Parents may post about your successes on social media. Coaches may elevate you above your teammates. You cannot control those things.

All you can control is how you respond to those things and how you view yourself.

Remember that you are more than an athlete. No matter how high you rise or how low you fall, you are still you.

Your strengths, abilities, and gifts do not change whether you are on top of the podium or riding the bench.

16. Energy Management for Less Stress and Better Performance, Part 1

Time management matters, but energy management changes the game.

Your time is limited but your energy is not. Have you ever seen a tired, sluggish, low-energy athlete be successful? Me neither.

You manage your *physical* energy through proper nutrition, exercise, and sleep.

You manage your *emotional* and *mental* energy through practices like taking time off, communicating your thoughts and feelings to others, mindfulness, surrounding yourself with energy givers not energy suckers, not saying "yes" to everything, and other similar habits.

Symptoms of Poor Energy Management

- Always tired
- Performance dropping
- No motivation
- Getting moody
- Trouble sleeping
- Getting sick or injured a lot
- Can't focus
- Relying on energy drinks
- Always sore
- Feeling drained
- Burned out
- Mental fog
- Feeling more stressed

Are you experiencing any of those? Keep reading, Part 2 will help you get on track!

17. Energy Management for Less Stress and Better Performance, Part 2: Mastering Transitions

Sonya was a 13-year-old athlete who was starting to achieve big time success in swimming, but she was exhausted everyday and never had energy for friends, homework, or other things that were important to her.

Sonya did not know how to take time to **mentally transition** from activity to activity. She would go from home to school, from class to class, from school to practice, from practice to home, from dinner to school work, and then pass out without transitioning properly to bed.

A transition is when you pause, mentally or physically, in between events. This happens moment to moment throughout your day, as well as season to season.

You have to be *mindful* of these *moments* if you want to keep your energy high, be happier, *and* be more effective in whatever you are doing!

Sonya started to adopt the following **transition habits:**

1. Before she walked out her front door to head to the bus, she would pause for 20 seconds, close her eyes, take 5 deep breaths, and think about the 3 things she was most looking forward to that day.
2. In between classes, before rushing out of the classroom, she would sit for 15 seconds or so to simply think about what she just learned in that class and which class she was headed to next.
3. After school, she *had* to rush to get to practice on time. But she still wanted to have a *mindful transition*. So, she began a habit of walking quickly with a friend and having a meaningful, fulfilling conversation.

4. The transition from practice to home used to be brutal. That's when her moodiness with her mom would kick in, because she was mentally and physically exhausted from a day full of *no transitions*.

To ensure she was happy and positive for her family, she wanted to have another planned transition at this point of the day. Rather than scrolling social media on the car ride home while simultaneously becoming increasingly annoyed as mom asked her questions, Sonya started to take a 15 minute nap on the car ride home instead. Her mom obviously supported this!

Whoa. What a game changer. Because of these transitions throughout her day, which *anyone can do*, Sonya had plenty of energy to complete her homework at night. Plus, she was able to complete it faster and with greater accuracy because she was more focused.

Are you seeing how energy management and transitions will completely transform your energy, performance, and entire life? I hope so. Head to part 3 for the final tips on energy management.

18. Energy Management for Less Stress and Better Performance, Part 3: Transitioning From Season to Season

Remember the symptoms of poor energy management from part 1?

Not *all* of them can be solved by day-to-day, moment-to-moment, transitions. You must master the art of transitioning well season-to-season.

Too many athletes are burning out and breaking down because they have ZERO mental or physical transitions between sports teams and sports seasons.

MINDSET, MOTIVATION, & MENTAL TOUGHNESS

Oftentimes, club sports tryouts overlap with your school sports seasons and vice versa. I know you cannot always control this but you can control how you transition mentally between seasons. Try these tips:

1. At the end of any season, make time to ask yourself the following questions:
   a) What went well this season?
   b) What did I learn?
   c) What could have gone better?
   d) What can I appreciate about this season? (This could be regarding teammates, team culture, and your own mindset and performance.)
2. Schedule a sports massage or a stretch at a local stretching studio.
3. Take a day to do something fun that makes you happy. Go snowboarding with friends, go to the movies, or do whatever else would be fun and engaging. Don't just sit around at home and play videogames or scroll social media. Plan something for a full day that will help you get *out* of sports mode and into *fun and renewal mode.*

It's time to take action. Start planning out how you will apply these energy management tips!

19. Staying Present: The Power of WIN

To wrap up the section on Mindset and Motivation, I want to cover a topic that causes so many young athletes frustration. The inability to stay present is painful for athletes all the way from middle school to the college level.

Focus on W.I.N to be in the NOW

W.I.N. = What's Important Now

EVERYTHING YOUNG ATHLETES SHOULD KNOW

When you are at home at the dinner table, family is most important.

When a friend of yours is going through a tough time, being present and encouraging that friend is the most important thing in that moment - not doing extra skill work to get ahead of the competition.

When you are at practice, being locked in on the drills and focusing on what the coach needs you to do is most important - not talking with your friends about tonight's plans.

When you are in the gym, working out as strong and hard as you can is the most important thing - not sending messages to friends or scrolling social media.

When you are doing homework, focusing on setting yourself up for future academic success is the most important thing – not calling a friend or shopping for new shoes online.

When you are stretching and foam rolling, recovering from your workout is the most important thing.

The problem is that we have so many opportunities to get distracted. If you want to be more present, you have to take the appropriate steps and eliminate distractions. Try these following things:

1. Put the phone out of sight when you are with family or friends
2. Talk about practice and sports related things at practice
3. Sit away from your friends in class if you are tempted to talk to them
4. Write your workouts on paper instead of on your phone
5. Confront your fear of falling behind which causes you to be in the future too often

MINDSET, MOTIVATION, & MENTAL TOUGHNESS

6. Repeat the phrases: "Focus, focus, focus," or "I am present, I am present, I am present."

7. Ask the following question every single day, multiple times a day: "WIN- what's important now?"

You are on your way to having a better mindset, being more motivated, and being more present. Now, let's get into category 2 which is all about Goal Setting and Achievement.

THE SECOND
ESSENTIAL AREA OF MASTERY

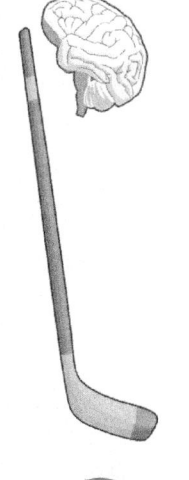

DREAMING BIG AND ACHIEVING IMPOSSIBLE GOALS

20. 4 Critical Errors in Goal-Setting That Can Cost You

Courtney was a 16-year-old swimmer who was beyond frustrated with the way she had been performing.

In her last meet she had swam a 1:08 in her 100 meter freestyle.

"What was your goal, Courtney?" I asked.

She replied, "I mean, I didn't necessarily have one but I hit 1:07 last meet so I should have swam a 1:06. But, I didn't. So now I am mad and I don't even know if I'll be able to get a state cut time next year."

Prior to swimming the 1:07 in the meet a few weeks before, Courtney had swam a personal best of 1:09.

In her head, she thought she needed to do better than the meet before at every single meet.

That is not a wise way to "set goals". That *is* a sure way to be discouraged more often than you are encouraged.

4 Critical Errors When Setting Goals

1. **Not Writing Them Down.** This is lazy! It's easy to do, but also easy *not to do*.
2. **Making them vague.** "Have a great season," is open to interpretation. And since you are your worst critic, that interpretation is almost never good.
3. **Copying someone else's goals.** Comparison will rob you of joy and the motivating feeling of progress. Instead, you need to own your goals and unique, personal reasons why you want to achieve them!

4. **Putting all your eggs in one "goal" basket.** In a future chapter I'll teach you how to set multi-tier goals in addition to your big goal.

This is important because when you only have one huge goal, you limit yourself to feeling successful only if you hit that one big goal.

Now, let's move on to the benefits of goal setting.

21. The Power of Goal Setting: Key Benefits Explained, Part 1

Benefit #1: Having goals gives you FOCUS, and focus is the most powerful force in your world.

Have you ever had a time in your sports career where you were not motivated or excited?

Think back to those times. Did you have clear, motivating, short-range goals that you were working toward for that season? Or, did you just have some big, far out goal like "get a scholarship someday?"

When you have a target in sight that you can see and aim for, you are immediately more motivated.

Benefit #2: Having goals protects you from comparison.

I have talked with many athletes who are more focused on others accomplishments than their own goals.

"My best friend got first team all conference and I am mad that I didn't."

"Ok, but what was *your* goal at the beginning of the season?"

"That girl is scoring 15 points a game and I am only scoring 10."

"Ok, but what is *your* goal?"

"The pole vaulter from that other school is jumping 13 feet! I wish I could do that."

"Ok, but what is going to be *your* goal for this season? By the end of the season, what would progress look like for *you*?"

When you have something to aim at, you are not looking to the left at that person, or to the right at the other person.

You are locked in on what matters most to you!

22. The Power of Goal Setting: Key Benefits Explained, Part 2

Benefit #3: Having goals protects you from the effects of criticism (self criticism and criticism from others)

Setting short-range goals consistently will keep you not only from being overly critical of yourself in an unhelpful way, but it will actually protect you from being negatively impacted by the criticism of others.

Every once in a while, a teammate or even a coach may critique your results and make you feel like you are not as far along as you should be.

Sure, criticism can be a helpful tool that you can use as fuel.

However, when you have clear goals for yourself at the beginning of the season and you know them like the back of your hand, that criticism would not have affected you nearly as much.

Why is that?

Because you may very well be *on track* to eventually achieving them, even if you have not arrived at the destination quite yet. When you don't have clear goals for the season, then any setback or bad performance may cause you to overreact instead of pausing and saying to yourself, "It's all good. I am still on track for my season goals."

Benefit #4: Having consistent, clear goals keeps you motivated when adversity strikes

Imagine you roll your ankle and you are out for 2 weeks. For an athlete who does not have goals for their season, he or she may become discouraged and make it a bigger deal than it should be.

However, if you have 90 day goals, you can have peace of mind and confidence that you still have 11 more weeks to work toward the things that matter most to YOU this season.

Goals, both short and long term, will motivate you when a major or minor setback arises. Athletes who get injured and their mental health plummets, for example, would have felt better if they had set multiple tiers of goals.

Before I teach you how to set your 90 day goals, there are two prerequisites that must happen to prepare yourself.

23. The Art of Successful Goal Setting, Part 1: Defining Your "Becoming" Goals

Becoming Goals are the "goals before the goals" that will lead you to accomplishing the tangible goals that you set.

If you want to be the leading scorer on your team and score 20 goals this season, what type of player do you need to *become* that you are not currently being today?

EVERYTHING YOUNG ATHLETES SHOULD KNOW

Let's imagine that the coach has been telling you lately that you are a little too passive. You are not *aggressive* enough.

Let's also imagine that in games, you lose focus quickly and get distracted. When you shoot, the ball often goes high or wide. Your inability to lock in and *focus* is holding you back.

And finally, let's pretend that last season you repeatedly gave up on yourself and decided you would just be a great assist man or woman when you were not scoring the ball well. You weren't *persistent* enough.

In the situation above, your **Becoming Goals** might be as follows:

- Aggressive
- Focused
- Persistent

Now what I want you to do is put the words "I AM" in front of each of those words, and then set a reminder for yourself daily, 1 to 3 times per day, and read the statements out loud.

- "I AM AGGRESSIVE."
- "I AM FOCUSED."
- "I AM PERSISTENT."

Remember, before you set performance goals, you need to figure out who you need to *become* in order to reach those goals!

> "You can have more than you've got because you can become more than you are."
>
> - JIM ROHN

24. The Art of Successful Goal Setting, Part 2: Creating Your BHAG

A BHAG (Big Hairy Audacious Goal) is a goal that is a minimum of 1 year out, and a maximum of 5 years away. It is your "north star" that is so bright and exciting that you can't stop thinking about it or looking at it. It is the thing you've been dreaming about for a long time.

Before I teach you how to do it I want to know, what's got you fired up? What excites you, scares you, makes you ask, "Is that even possible?"

You may be thinking, "why should I even write that dream down? It seems so impossible."

I want you to shift that thinking and instead ask, "Why not?"

Why not?

It's time to dream big. It's time to be bold.

Now, there are 3 parts to establishing your BHAG:

1. WHAT is it?
2. WHY do you want it?
3. HOW will you achieve it?

Step 1: WHAT is your big goal?

Examples:

- To make my varsity team and become a captain
- To run a sub 4 minute mile
- To swim a sub 1 minute in the 100 meter fly and earn a scholarship

EVERYTHING YOUNG ATHLETES SHOULD KNOW

Take some time to really think about your big goal.

My BHAG: _____

Step 2: WHY do you want it?

Why-Power is > Will-Power.

The bigger the goal, the more important the "Why"! Sarah is a young swimmer that I did mindset coaching for.

- ➤ **Sarah's "What":** I want to break 1 minute in my 100 meter fly.
- ➤ **Sarah's Why:** "It's my challenge. It's going to push me to stay committed and consistent. It's not about being "the best" or "better than others." I want that feeling of accomplishment, of being proud of myself. I love creating an atmosphere for myself and my family where they get excited to see me go for big goals. If I don't hit it, it's not the end of the world. For me, this is about pushing toward a goal that will make me a BETTER version of myself in the process!"

Guess what? Sarah achieved her goal!

A lot of other swimmers had the same goal, but failed to achieve it. She achieved it because she had a deep, compelling reason why she wanted to achieve it. And she read her WHY daily!

What is your WHY? Write it in the space below:

_____

_____

_____

_____

25. The Art of Successful Goal Setting, Part 3: Developing a Clear Plan of Action

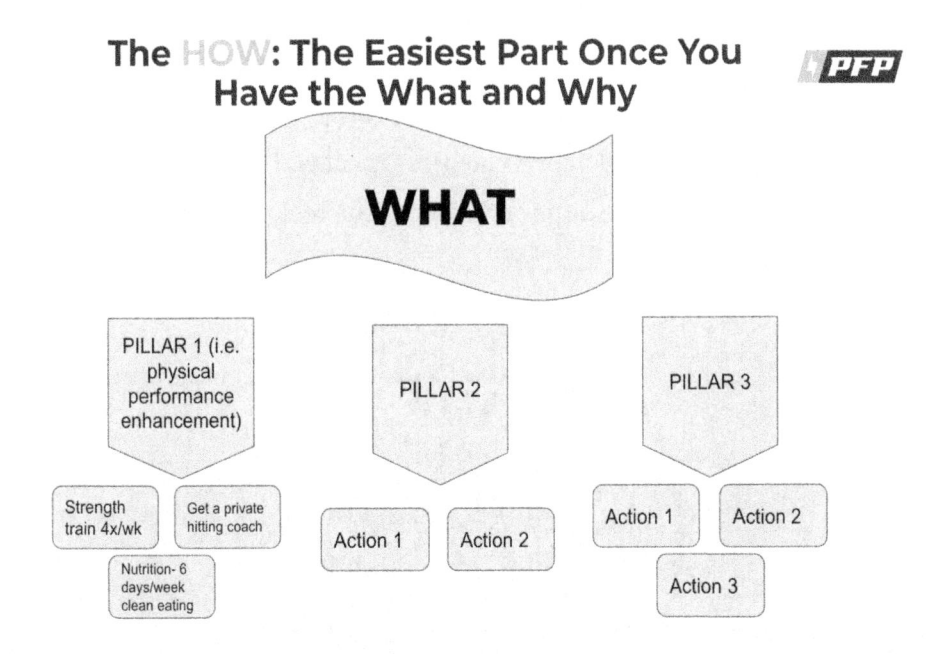

The HOW: The Easiest Part Once You Have the What and Why

```
                    WHAT

  PILLAR 1 (i.e.
    physical          PILLAR 2        PILLAR 3
  performance
  enhancement)

  Strength    Get a private                     Action 1   Action 2
  train 4x/wk hitting coach   Action 1  Action 2
  Nutrition- 6                                      Action 3
  days/week
  clean eating
```

The bigger the goal, the more thoughtful and thorough the plan for you to achieve it needs to be. The "*How*" includes the pillars (ideally 3 to 5) that are going to help you reach your "*What*," along with the specific action steps that go underneath that pillar.

EXAMPLE: If your "What" is to become a starter next season on your softball team, one pillar might be "physical performance." You are going to need to get stronger and improve your bat swing. The action steps are, "strength train 4x/week, get a private hitting coach, eat clean 6 days a week, and give up soda."

There may be others, but there are usually 3 big pillars and action steps. Now, go ahead and take some time to map out *your* pillars and action steps based on your big goal.

EVERYTHING YOUNG ATHLETES SHOULD KNOW

Now that you have your Becoming Goals and your BHAG, we are ready to set your Short-Term 90 Day Goals!

> **BONUS:** below you can access the free training that I created for athletes like you, walking you through my exact process for goal setting and achievement. It is called "The Advanced Goal Setting Workshop for Serious Athletes".

26. Crafting Short-Term, Tiered Goals

At the time I am writing this, I have been working with a college athlete named Rachel on goal setting for the past 4 years. She has been the most consistent athlete I have ever had when it comes to making progress on her Becoming Goals, reflecting on her BHAG, and finally, setting and achieving 90 day goals.

Here is the overview of how 90 day goal setting should look. Prior to her season starting, we consistently do these 3 things:

1. Spend 15 minutes reflecting on the previous 90 days.

She talks out loud about how she has improved over the last 90 days, what some "wins" were for her, what happened with her goals, how she is different today that she was 90 days ago, and what did not go well (i.e. her "losses").

She then writes all of those things down on paper. Why?

Because writing creates clarity, and clarity precedes success.

2. Spend 15 minutes talking about the BHAG. Visualize it, see it clearly, and get excited about it.

She reflects and thinks to herself, "How did I make progress toward my BHAG over the last 90 days?"

She writes down all the ways in which she has made progress toward her BHAG.

3. Set 3-tier goals for the next 90 days

In the next chapter we are going to cover the exact system for setting 90 day goals.

Step 1 is to create your "survive" goals, step 2 is to create your "succeed" goals, and step 3 is to create your "transform" goals.

Let's dive in!

27. How to Craft Bottom Tier, "Survive" Goals

After Rachel and I reflect on the past season, re-think and re-write her "becoming goals", and re-clarify her BHAG, we then spend the next 10 minutes writing down what "surviving" would look like for her over the next 90 days.

I know, it's not very inspiring. But setting Survive Goals is important because it gives you a baseline to build off of.

Most athletes just set one category of goals based on what would be *ideal*. It's important to have *ideal goals,* but it's also dangerous because there are unknowns that pop up during a season in sports that you cannot always plan for. "Survive" goals give you a foundation upon which to build your bigger goals.

So here are some of Rachel's:

- Just bat .275 this season.
- I just start again like last season, but I don't really make progress.
- I just hit 5-7 home runs, same as last year.
- I am a good teammate but don't really go out of my way to lead others.
- As a team, we get to the conference championship.

It is important for you to recognize that some of *Rachel's* "Survive" goals may be "Succeed" goals for someone else.

You must throw comparison out the door and set goals based on:

- What happened last season for *you.*
- What *could* happen this season.

Survive goals are a lot of "just" and "same" goals. Same as last year, just enough, etc.

Practice setting those below. I promise you'll see why after 90 days.

My Survive Goals Are:

- ➤ _____
- ➤ _____
- ➤ _____

28. How to Craft Mid Tier, "Succeed" Goals

This is when it starts to get more motivating.

Succeed goals are the things that must happen this season for you to feel like you made progress from last year. These are the things that will make you feel like you were successful at the end of the season.

Succeed goals are largely within your control. You don't need luck for things to fall into place, for your coach to make a certain decision, etc.

As long as you stay focused, work diligently, and are strategic in your approaches, you can absolutely achieve your Succeed goals.

Example of Rachel's Succeed Goals:

- ➤ I batted .325 this season.
- ➤ I hit 15 home runs.
- ➤ I made 1st team all conference.
- ➤ I built relationships with multiple freshmen and helped them get better.
- ➤ I was a captain again and used my position to influence the culture.
- ➤ I made the Dean's list.

EVERYTHING YOUNG ATHLETES SHOULD KNOW

In comparison to her results last year, these goals would be definite progress for her.

Notice how her Succeed goals were written *before* the season even started?

She wrote them like she had already achieved them. This is how you will want to write your "Succeed" and "Transform" goals.

As Rachel reads these everyday, her subconscious starts to believe that they had already happened!

My Succeed Goals Are:

- ➢ _____
- ➢ _____
- ➢ _____

29. How to Craft Top Tier, "Transform" Goals

Rachel set the following "Transform" goal before her sophomore season:

"*I made SportsCenter Top 10 Plays.*" To her, this was nearly impossible.

All the stars would have to align for this goal to become a reality. It was so far outside her control that she could not put it down as a "Succeed" goal.

But guess what?

It happened! TWICE!

She made SportsCenter Top 10 Plays two times during her sophomore season. Let's just say she quickly became a believer in setting "Transform" goals.

DREAMING BIG AND ACHIEVING IMPOSSIBLE GOALS

Transform goals are largely outside of your control and you'll likely need some luck, grace, and/or divine intervention for them to happen. But they are still worth writing down!

Examples:

> ➢ I scored 20 goals.
> ➢ I made 1st team all conference.
> ➢ Our team won states.

Write your goals in the space below.

My Transform Goals Are:

> ➢ _____
> ➢ _____
> ➢ _____

Now that you know how to set goals, it's time to move onto a critically important part of being a successful athlete: *maximizing your physical performance.*

THE THIRD
ESSENTIAL AREA OF MASTERY

PHYSICAL SKILLS, STRENGTH, SPEED, AND STAMINA:

HOW TO TRAIN HARD, SMART, & MAXIMIZE PHYSICAL ATHLETICISM FOR ANY SPORT

30. Overview: Performance Training and Skill Development

This is a loaded topic for young athletes. There are so many ways to improve your physical skills and performance. Here are a few more things athletes should understand if they are going to reach their full potential:

- ➢ Hiring a performance coach vs. doing it on my own
- ➢ Training for looks vs. training for performance
- ➢ Getting stronger
- ➢ Improving endurance and stamina
- ➢ Getting faster
- ➢ Improving balance
- ➢ Becoming more powerful and explosive
- ➢ Increasing flexibility and mobility
- ➢ Sport specific training
- ➢ Acquiring, developing, and maximizing your skills

There are a lot of things that athletes need to know about maximizing their performance training and skills in sports, but where do you start?

In this section and the chapters that follow, we are going to go over EVERYTHING you should know if you want to become the best you can be!

31. Hiring a Performance Coach vs. Doing it on Your Own

One big decision athletes need to make with their parents is how you are going to allocate your time and money to optimize your performance and set yourself up to achieve your big goals.

PHYSICAL SKILLS, STRENGTH, SPEED, AND STAMINA

You *could* spend $3,500 on a week-long tournament. You *could* spend $1,500 on a big showcase. Or, you could pay the same and train 2x/week with a personal trainer for an entire year. It's important to think long term, not just what feels good right now.

"Don't give up what you want *most* for what you want *now*," is a wise quote to guide your future decisions.

Athletes who invest in a personal trainer end up performing at a higher level and reaching bigger goals than athletes who do not.

Why? Here are the top 3 Reasons:

1. **Accountability and Goal Setting**. Ever have days you just *don't feel like it*? We all do. Having a trainer will keep you accountable to the action steps that matter most, whether you want to do it or not!

2. **Form Correction.** I have seen it a million times. Athletes *thought* their form was solid. But in reality, there was so much room for improvement - they just needed a coach to watch them. Slight adjustments, like making sure you are symmetrical on your deadlift, add up to produce huge results.

3. **Tempo, Pace, and Rest Intervals.** Very, very few athletes will naturally take the amount of time in between sets or reps that they need in order to maximize the benefit of that movement. Many either wait too long or do not wait long enough in between sets, resulting in decreased benefit from that move.

Having a trainer will ensure you are optimizing your rest-to-work ratios and that you are going at the speed/tempo that will result in the best outcomes based on your goals!

32. Things You Should Know Before You Invest in a Personal Trainer

1. Know their Track Record.

How many people like you have this trainer actually helped achieve the specific result that you are after? Do they have a substantial number of credible reviews? A lot of trainers get proud about the letters behind their name but I recommend finding a trainer who's proven to help athletes reach their goals in a safe and efficient way.

2. Do they provide real accountability?

The most important thing that will help you reach your goals is what you do during the 165 hours that you aren't in the gym. Make sure to ask the trainer how they will go about providing you with true accountability so that you stay motivated, consistent, and on track.

3. Are they there to SELL you or SERVE you?

Your trainer should be focused on you and your success. Look for an honest trainer who tells you the truth: that it will take many months of consistent effort for you to achieve your goals. "6-pack in 6-weeks" is a lie.

4. Do they understand sports movements?

There is a big difference between personal trainers and performance coaches. Personal trainers may understand how to help you lose weight or put on muscle, but performance coaches know how strength, speed, power, and all other types of exercises will benefit you in your individual sport.

5. Will they help you out with off day workouts?

A trainer providing their clients with off day workouts and guidance should be a common courtesy if the trainer is really invested in your success.

PHYSICAL SKILLS, STRENGTH, SPEED, AND STAMINA

6. Do they provide nutrition guidance and have nutrition resources? Or do they just say it to sell you?

Nutrition is paramount to success. Ask the trainer if they will help you with your nutrition, and then follow up with them after you sign up! Ask for more and they will give more; coaches and trainers are givers by nature – take advantage!

33. How to Build Serious Strength

In order to build serious strength, the kind of strength that is immovable and can move anything *it* desires, you need three things:

1. A solid, stable, mobile foundation to build on
2. Consistent, progressive overload: make it a little harder each time
3. The discipline to rest

Strength comes before speed.

Just as a car can only go so fast with its current engine, *you* can only go as fast as your current size muscles will allow. Building muscle is like putting a bigger engine in your car. It changes *everything*.

1. A solid, stable, mobile foundation to build on

A huge mistake athletes make is trying to keep up with your friends in the weight room. Be smart and make *your* priority having great form. Building strength on top of a dysfunctional foundation is a recipe for disaster.

When squatting, for example, can you get down to 90 degrees and keep a straight upper back with just your own bodyweight? If so, move to step 2.

2. Consistent, progressive overload

Again, having a trainer will help because he or she will tell you when you have mastered the step you are on and you are ready to move to the next.

A trainer will also make sure you are doing the amount of reps you need to do before moving to a new number of reps. An example of a progressive strength program is:

- **Weeks 1-3:** 2-3 sets of 15 reps
- **Weeks 4-6:** 3 sets of 12 reps
- **Weeks 7-9:** 4 sets of 8-10 reps
- **Weeks 10-12:** 4 sets of 6 reps
- **Weeks 13-15:** 5 sets of 4 reps (usually for older, more experienced lifters)

Each week, the goal would be to move up in weight. This is called "progressive overload". But remember, lifting weights is breaking *down* your muscles. The only way they will grow to be stronger as a result of lifting is if you do step 3.

3. The discipline to rest

Muscles do not grow when you are lifting weights. They grow when you are *resting.*

Take 2-3 days minimum in between exercising a certain part of your body and make sure to take 1 week off of heavy lifting every 12-14 weeks. If your muscles are not growing stronger and you are lifting all the time, that's the problem.

Lift heavy and go hard, but then rest.

34. Becoming Powerful and Explosive

I mentioned before that strength comes before speed. Actually, strength comes before power, and power comes before speed.

Many athletes make the mistake of *only* lifting heavy instead of also aiming to move as quickly as they can through the strength movement, while maintaining great form.

If your goal is to jump higher, hit the ball further, spike the ball with more force, swim faster, or serve harder, getting stronger alone will not help you *maximize* those movements. You must develop *power*.

Training for power is quite simple:

Perform your movements in the gym as fast as you can while maintaining good form.

Doing squats? Control it on the way down, *explode* on the way up.

Push ups? Control your body on the way down, *explode* through the ground on the way up.

Split squats? Same thing, just on one leg.

The phrase to remember while you are in the weight room is this: *Load and Explode.*

Some examples of great POWER exercises:

- **Baseball/softball**: side tosses into the wall with a medicine ball
- **Volleyball/basketball**: squat jumps with or without a weight
- **Tennis/volleyball serve**: overhead med ball throws into a wall
- **Swimming**: lunge jumps with or without weight
- **Hockey**: ice skater jumps

Move fast, move powerfully. You are an athlete who plays sports, not a bodybuilder!

35. Training for Looks Vs. Performance

Athlete, you have to decide– is your #1 goal to look big, fit, and muscular, or is your number one goal to perform at your full potential?

Those two goals are at odds with one another most of the time.

In reality, you *will* look strong, fit, and athletic if you train like an athlete.

But you will not *be* athletic to the level you are capable of if you train like a bodybuilder.

Athletes, especially young athletes, should focus on doing total body exercises and movements that incorporate multiple muscle groups at one time.

Bicep curls, tricep extensions, pec flies, shoulder raises, leg extensions, and other exercises that isolate one muscle group in one plane of motion only are not *bad,* but they should come at the very end of your workout *after* you've focused intensely on doing exercises that are wholesome and athletic.

I trained an athlete named Taylor who went on to play at a top-tier Division 1 school for lacrosse. Some of her friends would poke fun at her because her quad muscles were twice the size of theirs. But they weren't laughing when she got a full ride scholarship to a national championship caliber lacrosse school!

Insecurity vs. Confidence

Athlete, you are already impressive. You do not need to look a certain way or fit into the "perfect image" of what society says looks good. I've

PHYSICAL SKILLS, STRENGTH, SPEED, AND STAMINA

never met an athlete who became happier as a result of looking skinny (or big and strong, if that's your goal). It lasts for a moment, but then that feeling goes away.

I have met tons of athletes who trained hard to get stronger, more powerful, and athletic for their sport, which resulted in feeling more prepared and confident when it was game time.

Address your insecurities today - we all have them - then start training for performance first. The physique will take care of itself!

36. The Best Kept Secrets for Getting Faster

Above all other athletic qualities, speed is the one that can make the biggest, most immediate impact on your playing time, success, and chances of earning a college scholarship. Improving your speed can set you apart and get you noticed.

I have a friend who went to the NFL Scouting Combine to try making a pro team. His first year, he ran a 4.81 forty yard dash. That's *not typically* fast enough to play linebacker for a pro team.

He first followed the steps from above: *have good form, progressively overload to get stronger, rest, and train powerfully during workouts.*

Then, he went to work on speed development.

Strength is key to improving speed, but there are many, many, many other ways to train yourself to get as fast as you possibly can.

One tip for you to get faster is to sprint more.

"Duh Andrew! I know that!"

No, I mean really sprinting and going as fast as your body will move when you "sprint" (swimming, running, swinging, cycling, etc.)

Another tip for you is to sprint *against* teammates or friends as often as possible. Nothing will train you to go faster like competition.

"But Andrew, I am an introvert."

Ok. What do you want more? To be the fastest athlete you can be? Or to feel comfortable?

The third tip is to actually hire a speed coach *or* research speed training exercises online. More on that in the next chapter.

37. 7 Advanced Tips for Improving Your Speed

Starting today, if all that you do is take these 7 tips and begin applying them to your speed training, I promise you that overtime you *will* become a next level athlete.

1. **Anything UNDER 10 seconds is speed, anything OVER is conditioning.** Most athletes believe the myth that "if you aren't tired, you aren't getting better." This is absolutely false when it comes to developing speed. That leads to tip #2:
2. **Take FULL advantage of recovery times.** In between speed training sets or explosiveness drills, you should truly rest and recover. Don't do other workouts or jump on your phone and scroll social media or send messages to people. Let your mind and body fully rest!
3. **If you are fatigued during sprinting, your brain won't allow you to get faster.** When you are doing speed training, you should not be fatigued. You should be moving your fastest! Which leads to #4…

PHYSICAL SKILLS, STRENGTH, SPEED, AND STAMINA

4. **You need to be moving at 95% + speed in order to get faster.** This is why earlier I recommended that you always have a buddy to sprint *against* when training for speed.

5. **If you are hurt, sore, or tired, a good option is to do skill work.** "Pushing past the pain," is not helpful for speed training. That's a different kind of toughness. If you are hurt, sore, or tired, you should work on your sport specific skills.

6. **If you aren't timing your sprints, you are wasting your time.** What gets measured gets improved! Have someone time you when you are sprinting. It's worth it so that you can measure your next run against your last!

7. **You *can* learn how to get faster, and mechanics are important.** It's not enough just to "try as hard as you can". As mentioned in chapter 36, mechanics matter. If you do not know about shin angles, knee drive, ground force production, and other important keys for speed, you should follow a professional program.

"Ok, I believe I can and should train my speed. But I don't have a trainer! What do I do!?!"

Coach Kyle Daggett has created a brand new **10 Week Scholarship Level Speed Program** for serious athletes who want to get faster.

You do not need a track or a bunch of equipment to develop blazing speed. All you need is focus, the desire to improve, and this 10 week, video-based speed program that you can start using at home, today.

EVERYTHING YOUNG ATHLETES SHOULD KNOW

Scan the QR code to get access to the exact program Coach Kyle uses to help collegiate athletes shave time off their sprints and develop the speed and power they needed to get noticed and get scholarships.

Use code ATHLETEBOOK to get 50% off

38. Improving Endurance and Stamina

Now that you are moving fast, it's time to train your body to sustain that speed for as long as possible!

This is speed endurance.

Running long distances at submaximal paces is not helpful for most sports, unless it's a part of your recovery.

Your goal in most sports is to go as fast as you can, for as long as you can. That's how you win!

PHYSICAL SKILLS, STRENGTH, SPEED, AND STAMINA

Speed Interval Training is a great way to train for this. Here is an example of a 4 week, 2 day per week endurance training plan for a high school soccer, basketball, or lacrosse player. Remember to always warm up for 10 minutes minimum before conditioning:

Week 1 Day 1 Workout:

- ☐ 5x 100 yard sprint
- ☐ 3x 60 yard shuttles (up 15 yards, back 15 yards twice)
- ☐ Sprint .25 miles

Week 1 Day 2 Workout:

- ☐ 1 mile sprint to walk–sprint 15 seconds, walk 10
- ☐ 5x :30 second shuffle (5 yards back and forth)

Week 2 Day 1 Workout:

- ☐ 6x 100 yard sprint with :30 rest in between
- ☐ 4x 60 yard shuttles (up 15 yards, back 15 yards twice) with :30 rest in between
- ☐ Sprint .25 miles

Week 2 Day 2 Workout:

- ☐ 1 mile sprint to walk–sprint 15 seconds, walk 10
- ☐ 6x :30 second shuffle (5 yards back and forth)
- ☐ .5 mile sprint to walk–sprint :30 walk :15

Week 3 Day 1 Workout:

- ☐ 7x 100 yard sprint with :25 second rest in between
- ☐ 5x 60 yard shuttles (up 15 yards, back 15 yards twice)

- ☐ Sprint .25 miles

Week 3 Day 2 Workout:

- ☐ 10 yard Shuffle to 40 yard turn and sprint- 6 times facing each direction with :30 in between each
- ☐ 3x 300 yard shuttle (25 yards down, 25 yards back x 6) with 1 minute rest in between each

Week 4 Day 1 Workout:

- ☐ 8x 100 yard sprint with :20 second rest in between
- ☐ 6x 60 yard shuttles (up 15 yards, back 15 yards twice)
- ☐ 3 rounds of side planks :30-:60 each side (until fatigue)

Week 4 Day 2 Workout:

- ☐ 10 yard shuffle to 40 yard turn and sprint- 6 times facing each direction with :30 in between each
- ☐ 4x 300 yard shuttle (25 yards down, 25 yards back x 6) with 1 minute rest in between each

Try this workout and remember to bring a friend, run as fast as you can, and then rest and recover!

39. Improving Rhythm, Balance, and Coordination

There might not be anything more important for a young athlete than to improve these three skills:

1. **Rhythm** is the expression of timing in movements.

PHYSICAL SKILLS, STRENGTH, SPEED, AND STAMINA

2. **Balance** is the ability to stay upright or stay in control of body movement.

3. **Coordination** is the ability to perform smooth, accurate, and controlled movements by using multiple parts of the body in a coordinated fashion.

How do you go about improving each of these?

1. **Play multiple sports.** In my book, *The Unstoppable Athlete*, I spent an entire chapter on this topic. Playing multiple sports as a young athlete is undeniably the best way to improve your rhythm, balance, and coordination, while also reducing risk of injury. And don't just play a bunch of sports where the movements are similar– try sports that require you to learn new ways to use your body!

2. **Get off the screens.** Get outside and play sports with your friends. Backyard football, pick up basketball, tag, race, playing on playgrounds, pick-up baseball or kickball, bike riding.

Athlete, you can do this. Choose now to break the pattern of screen addiction, be the leader your friends need you to be, and go make it happen!

40. Sport Specific Training

As mentioned before, it's important to play multiple sports. But, there are also specific movements you can be doing that will help you be better at those unique sports!

Examples of how sport specific movements occur:

> ➤ Lacrosse players who play attack should work on sprinting forward, drop step shuffling, spin moves, and then sprinting again.

EVERYTHING YOUNG ATHLETES SHOULD KNOW

> ➤ Basketball players should practice the art of being in a defensive stance with active feet, shuffling to the left or right as fast as possible, and closing out on a shot. This can all be done with band resistance in the gym!

Head back to chapter 37 and grab the 10 Week Scholarship Speed Program, which includes 100+ advanced speed training exercises for all athletes. In addition to movements, energy systems also need to be considered.

Examples of how sport specific energy systems are impacted:

> ➤ Baseball and softball players primarily rely on their anaerobic energy system, which is high power and short duration, because of the many start and stop movements in the game. However, due to this, baseball, softball, and other explosive athletes typically have low aerobic capacity, which is not good. Every athlete needs some level of endurance.

Baseball players should *primarily* train their anaerobic systems for short burst movements, but they also need to incorporate *some* cardio!

> ➤ Cross country athletes on the other hand rely primarily on their aerobic energy system, which is low power and long duration, because of the steady state movements. However, due to this, cross country, soccer, and other endurance athletes have low anaerobic abilities.

This is not good during the last leg of a race when you need to accelerate up to a higher gear to finish strong. Endurance athletes should *primarily* train aerobically, but they also need to incorporate power, speed, and strength so that they can dominate in the final moments or meters of a game or race!

41. From Talent to Mastery: Skill Development Specific to Your Sport

Working hard without working smart is a perfect pathway to poor performance. It's good to work hard on the skills you are already proficient in, but what other skills do you need to develop in order to reach your goals?

Skill development is the X-factor to becoming a "Master of ONE" instead of a "Jack of all trades".

The best athletes in the world know how to focus on developing *one skill at a time.*

Focus on skills like:

- ➢ Your defensive quickness in basketball
- ➢ Your forehand in tennis
- ➢ Your set in volleyball
- ➢ Your finish when throwing a shotput

It's boring, but boring *is* the pathway to mastery.

A chef who is going to become the top chef in the world does not work on mastering every type of cuisine at the same time. He or she spends months and oftentimes *years* honing the different types of dishes in a single cuisine before moving on to master another.

The same should be true for you in your sport! Sure, you can work on ball handling, shooting, and passing all in the same practice. But what are you giving the *majority, the best, of your attention, time, and energy to?*

At any given point in time, be prepared to answer the question, "What skill are you working to become a *master* in right now?"

"Ok, coach. I buy into this idea. But how do I know what skill is most important to develop next?"

Step 1: Identify what is your current greatest skill. Three point shooting? Spiking in volleyball? Serving in tennis? Your turn in the pool? Your backstroke? Make sure you "double click" on those strengths everyday and take them to the moon!

Step 2: Revisit your biggest goals. Based on those goals, what *other* skills are most important for you to develop in order to reach those goals?

Step 3: Ask your coach, parents, or teammates.

Step 4: Build a weekly plan that includes a minimum of 4 focused, intense, 30 minute sessions where you are working on that skill.

"Should I work on my weaknesses?"

Yes, but only to get those weaknesses up to an "acceptable baseline" for what your coach needs you to do and for what your future goals will require.

If your future goal is to be the best all around gymnast in the world, then you need to work on *every* type of routine– floor, beam, vault, and bars. But again, there should be one or two of those that you become the absolute master in.

We have weaknesses for a reason. Take your *strengths* to the moon and get your *weaknesses* up to where they need to be!

PHYSICAL SKILLS, STRENGTH, SPEED, AND STAMINA

42. Planning, Accountability, and Intensity

The final things an athlete needs to know when it comes to skill development are the following three things:

1. **A skill development plan:** Do you have one? If it is not written down on paper and in your calendar, it's not a plan!
2. **Accountability:** Do you have people who will help you do your skill development well, even on days you don't feel like it?
3. **"Hone Your How":** Consistency is *not* enough to reach your full potential. In my first book to coaches and parents called "The Youth Truth," I talk about a concept called "Honing Your How."

When I went to college my freshman year to play basketball, I thought I was in great shape. After all, I had worked out and played basketball five or six days a week for the entire summer, and for a long time leading up to that summer. I was very *consistent*.

When I got there, I noticed something about the *way* the upperclassmen were training, conditioning, recovering, and doing their skill development. Their *intensity* was different. It got me thinking, "What I am doing is good. *How* I am doing it is not going to cut it at the next level."

These guys were doing drills in a way that I had never seen, at an intensity I did not know existed. In addition, they had their teammates filming them during their drills. I thought this was a little crazy and over the top.

That is what people say who really don't want to change, put in more work, or do what is needed to become the BEST they can be. They say things like, "That's over-the-top."

If you want to become the best athlete you can be, avoid plateaus, experience *continual improvement,* and continually level up your results, it will take *far more* than practicing five days a week for two hours a day, year after year.

You will need to pay attention to *how* you train, the *intensity* with which you train, and then do that consistently day after day, week after week, year after year!

THE FOURTH
ESSENTIAL AREA OF MASTERY

FUELING LIKE A GOLD MEDALIST:
NUTRITION AND HYDRATION DOS AND DON'TS

43. Overview: Nutrition and Fueling for Performance

Our athletes say they struggle with 2 things when it comes to nutrition:

1. **Competence**: Knowing *what* they should be eating or drinking, *when* they should eat it, and *what* specifically to avoid
2. **Motivation** and **Discipline**: *Making good choices*

Here are the 6 real reasons you struggle with nutrition:

1. Bad Influences.
2. No immediate consequences.
3. Bad food tastes better, duh!
4. Change is hard and if you don't see a real reason, it makes more sense to stay put.
5. Lack of knowledge and clear direction; not having a specific game-plan or guidance.
6. Not having a strong "why" to change.

Why change? Why eat and drink better? Why hydrate more? Why should you be concerned about the timing of when you eat or drink?

Let's dive deep into the problems as well as the solutions for you to ensure you are fueling your body like a champion. But first, take a second to write down your BIG goals and dreams again for your sport:

My Big, Hairy, Audacious Goal (BHAG) in Sports is:

_____

_____

_____

_____

44. Nutrition and The Law of the Path

The first and most important reason for you to level up your eating habits is this: The law of the path states that you are currently on a path, and that path will lead you somewhere.

Think about the path you are currently on with your nutritional habits…where does that path lead? Chronic injuries? Dehydration? Broken bones in sports because of too much soda and not enough vegetables?

You might need to hop on a new path. Here are a few questions to get you going:

1. Do you want to play college sports?
2. Are you sick of getting knocked down and knocked around due to not being able to keep muscle on? Possibly as a result of poor nutrition?
3. Are you tired of coming up short constantly in games?
4. Is your endurance suffering?
5. Do you struggle with focusing, paying attention, or having enough energy in school or sports?

Eating healthier and eating enough will help with *all* of these!

For the next 4 chapters I am bringing in my friend Sarah Stack. Sarah is the author of *The Teenage Athletes' Nutrition Journal* and is an expert on this topic. Enjoy, and take notes!

45. Don't Be Fooled! Reading Nutrition Labels and Ingredient Lists | By: Sarah Stack

In order to make healthy food choices, you first have to buy healthy food from the grocery store. That is where knowing how to understand nutrition labels and ingredient lists comes into play.

EVERYTHING YOUNG ATHLETES SHOULD KNOW

While the front of food packaging is designed to capture your attention, the nutrition facts label and ingredients list, found on either the side or back of the food box or bag, contains the facts: the good, the bad and the ugly!

When you are grocery shopping, ignore the front of the box, and look immediately at the nutrition label and the ingredients list. The front of the box may have misleading words such as the name of a fruit, or the words "sugar free."

A fruit name on a food product does not mean that that product actually contains that fruit! It could simply contain an artificial flavor additive so that the food tastes like the fruit indicated on the front of the box.

The words "sugar free" printed on the front of a food package are a red flag for artificial sweeteners. Always look at the ingredient list to see what sugar substitute is used to sweeten the food.

Here are the main points to remember when reading a nutrition label.

- ➢ Take note of the serving size!
- ➢ Your macros (fats, carbohydrates, and protein) will be in bold print.
- ➢ Notice the sugar content! If it is low, read the ingredient list to see if there is an artificial sweetener or natural sugar alternative used. If most of the total sugar is added sugar, take note. Natural sugars are better than added sugar.
- ➢ High fiber foods (more than 5 grams) are great; look for this category under the carbohydrate section.

You will frequently hear people talk about the number of calories in a food rather than how nutritious a food is or is not. If you pay attention to the macros, fiber, sugar, and saturated fat, the calories will take care of themselves!

Additionally, not all calories are created equally. Eating a 100 calorie snack pack of cookies is not the same as eating 100 calories of fresh fruit.

The ingredients list is usually printed under or next to the nutrition facts label *in tiny print*. The ingredients are listed in order based on the amount of each ingredient in the food item. So, if sugar and sunflower seed oil are listed at the beginning of the list, the food item contains a lot of sugar and sunflower seed oil.

> ➤ Steer clear of foods with ingredients that are hard to pronounce, gums, and artificial preservatives and dyes. These slow athletes down.
> ➤ Generally speaking, the longer the ingredients list, the more processed the food item is. High-performing athletes eat whole foods!

Following these simple guidelines when grocery shopping will help keep your pantry stocked with healthy and nutritious food that will move you toward accomplishing your goals!

Sample nutrition label from: https://www.fda.gov/food/food-labeling-nutrition/changes-nutrition-facts-label

46. Hydration Essentials | By: Sarah Stack

The water in your body has an important job, especially during exercise. It helps cool you down - by sweating! Sweat comes from the water in your blood, and it keeps your body from overheating.

When you sweat a lot, you lose that water, making your blood thicker. This makes your heart work harder to pump blood, which can make you tired and lower your energy. If you want to perform better and feel less tired, you need to be hydrated!

You should make an effort to be well hydrated prior to exercising. Drink half of your pounds of body weight in ounces daily, then add 15 oz.

My Bodyweight: _____ lbs / 2 = _____ + 15 oz = _____

Generally speaking, drinking 8-16 ounces of water per hour during exercise is sufficient for maintaining fluid levels.

Dehydration Effects

About 15 minutes into a conditioning session, Ella stopped and gasped "I feel so sluggish, Coach Sarah! Why is this so hard today?"

I immediately asked her how much water she had consumed that day, and what she had to eat at lunch and before her session.

She had a reasonable lunch, and a snack bag of crackers before her session, but most notable was her admission that she had only had a few sips of water at lunch and a few sips more with her snack.

Can you relate?

She continued to complain that her school requires students to bring a clear water bottle, rather than an insulated water bottle, so her water couldn't stay cold. She felt that she'd drink more water during the day if she could drink cold water instead of the room temperature water that she carried around in her clear plastic water bottle.

I understood her dilemma, and she understood the importance of drinking enough water, but we still had a problem to solve. She had no control over the fact that clear plastic water bottles were required at her school.

Because this was out of her control, we were not going to expend our energy complaining about it. Instead, we came up with a plan so that she could drink enough water daily without having to rely on room temperature water at school. Her goal for the day was to drink 75 ounces of water each day.

That's step one: know your goal!

She decided she would drink between 16-20 ounces of cold water in the morning before she left for school.

Next, she realized that she could fill her water bottle with a lot of ice in the morning, and top off the ice from the fountain drink machine at lunch, which would get her through most of her day having access to cold water. Solutions!

On days when she had practice after school she could stop back at the ice machine and top off her water bottle again. On days that she didn't have practice she could go home and switch to an insulated water bottle for the rest of the day.

After a few days of putting our simple plan into action and drinking 75 ounces of cold water each day, she reported back that she did not "fatigue out" in her workouts or in practice, and that she was visiting the bathroom more often (which is of course a side effect of prioritizing hydration!)

47. The Truth About Sports Drinks | By: Sarah Stack

Sports drinks have their place, but they are not needed in every exercise situation. They are advisable if you're engaging in prolonged exercise (at least an hour) in a hot environment.

A 45 minute weight lifting session in an air conditioned gym is not prolonged exercise in a hot environment. However, a two hour long soccer practice on an outdoor field in July does indeed count as prolonged exercise in a hot environment.

Not all sports drinks are created equally! Pay attention to the nutrition facts label and ingredients list when choosing a sports drink. The key ingredients to notice are the electrolytes, like sodium and potassium, carbohydrates, and sugar content.

For an 8 oz serving you want to see:

- ➢ 100 mg of sodium and 20 mg of potassium. Sodium helps your body hold on to the water rather than sweating it out, and the potassium is the vehicle for the sodium to be distributed throughout your body.
- ➢ 7-10 g of carbs, which is energy replenishment fuel.
- ➢ No more than 10 g of sugar. Sugar is another vehicle for the sodium to be distributed throughout your body, but excess sugar in any form is detrimental.

In addition to knowing what *to* look for in a sports drink, you should also familiarize yourself with what you *do not* want to see in your sports drink nutrition label and ingredient list.

Those items include sucralose or other artificial sweeteners. Stevia and monk fruit are much better alternatives!

48. Quick Tips and Swaps to Fuel Performance
By: Sarah Stack

I'll leave you with this: improving nutritional habits doesn't have to be difficult or complicated.

Here are some easy-to-implement tips and healthy swaps that can make a big impact.

The following bullet points list out some simple rules to follow to help you make healthy nutritional choices:

- Add a plant to every meal.
- Eat a natural source of fiber, such as fresh fruits and vegetables, daily.
- Build your meal around the protein, then add in veggies, fruits, and grains.
- Drink water throughout your day to stay well hydrated. Invest in a water bottle that helps to make it easier to drink the recommended amount of water daily
- Limit added sugar. Most sugar substitutes are better alternatives than sucralose.
- Eat from a salad bar when one is available.
- Limit baked goods, fried foods, candy, and soda.

EVERYTHING YOUNG ATHLETES SHOULD KNOW

> ➤ Pack a cooler with your lunch and healthy snacks such as fresh fruit, cheese sticks, raw veggies with greek yogurt ranch dip or hummus, turkey sandwich on whole grain bread, or a PB&J sandwich on whole grain bread.
>
> ➤ Don't sweat a bad choice. It's done, there's nothing you can do about it and stressing about it, or being upset with yourself about it, will not change the fact that you ate it. Eat it, enjoy it, and move on!

Here are some easy healthy swaps to make:

Sugar	Stevia, monk fruit, no added sugar applesauce
Pasta	Spaghetti squash, lentil pasta, whole wheat pasta
Mayo	Greek yogurt, hummus, mashed avocado
Canned Vegetables	Frozen vegetables
Creamy Salad Dressing	Homemade vinaigrette
Dessert	Yogurt, fruit, granola, protein shake
White Bread	Whole wheat bread, lettuce wraps
Potatoes	Sweet potatoes

Now that you are better equipped to make wiser nutritional choices, let's dive into the 5th essential area of mastery for every young athlete.

THE FIFTH
ESSENTIAL AREA OF MASTERY

RECOVERY, SLEEP, & INJURY PREVENTION:

THE UNSEEN HABITS OF THE BEST ATHLETES ON THE PLANET

49. Recovery and Sleep: Habits of the Best Athletes on the Planet

Who wants to be the most strong, talented, prepared, explosive athlete *on the bench* because of an injury that could have been prevented?

I know that does not sound fun, but unfortunately this becomes true for many athletes. I want to make sure that isn't you.

Recovery and sleep are two of the most important activities you should master because they:

1. Decrease your risk of injury
2. Maximize your performance
3. Help you stay mentally healthy

In this section we are going to cover some habits of the best athletes in the world, why sleep matters, and how to get excellent quality sleep so that you can perform like a champion.

If you are going to play and train like a professional athlete, you have to embrace recovery and rest like one too!

50. The Power of Sleep: How Missing Rest Impacts Your Growth

As mentioned in the chapter on "building strength", your muscles do not grow when you are working out or training.

They grow when you are resting.

It's a bunch of boring, science type stuff but essentially, there are small muscle fibers that *tear apart* when you are running, jumping, throwing, lifting weights, etc.

RECOVERY, SLEEP, & INJURY PREVENTION

It takes time for those fibers to repair themselves and get them back to full strength.

If you do not give them proper time to rest, and you do not do activities that help *speed up* the repairing process, you are going to go back to playing your sport and further tear the same fibers that are still torn!

That's when pulled muscles, ankle sprains, and other injuries happen. Ouch!

Working out, lifting weights, and skills training are completely useless if you do not sleep well. I wish there was an easier way, but there's not. You *must* get better sleep.

Here are the things that affect your sleep quality:

1. Unresolved relationship issues: This leads to "tossing and turning" at night, overthinking, and not getting into a deep sleep.
2. Unresolved insecurities, anxiety, and fear: This is similar to the one above, but may not be about relationships. These insecurities could be due to school work, a presentation, or upcoming competitions.
3. Overstimulating your brain too close to bed: Being on video games, your phone, television, or the computer too close to bedtime.

Which ones most apply to you and your situation right now?

_____

_____

_____

_____

EVERYTHING YOUNG ATHLETES SHOULD KNOW

What is your goal for hours of quality sleep per night? (Hint: It should be 7 hours minimum.)

_____ hours

Now, let's dive into the simple solutions for improving your sleep. These will require sacrifice and dedication to your big goals. Are you ready?

51. Building Healthy Sleep Habits, Part 1

Here are the solutions to improving your sleep:

1. Resolving your relationship issues.

The one thing we all have in common, whether we are 8 years old, 18, or 80, is that relationships are the best thing in our lives *and* the most difficult.

I have a rule: *never let the sun go down on my anger*. This means that I never go to sleep with an unresolved disagreement between me and another person, especially people I love. Unfortunately, those people are often the hardest people to apologize to or reconcile with.

Become quick to resolve arguments, disagreements, or frustrations you have with family members, teammates, friends, etc. This will positively affect your quality of sleep which affects your muscles and your performance! Call the person, text them, or grab them before you or they leave school or practice. Be brave and always aim to restore the relationship quickly.

2. Resolving your anxiety and fear.

If you are anxious about an upcoming event, test, or game, you need a way to get those thoughts *out of your head* so that you can face them and replace the lies with truth. *Talk them through with a parent, write them down, or pray about them.* Do not let them sit in your mind and fester!

If you have big fears that are causing you to hesitate, sleep poorly, and worry constantly, what would you recommend your best friend do? *Talk to someone,* of course.

F.E.A.R. is nothing more than False Evidence Appearing Real.

Anxiety is focusing on *what might happen* in the future.

In "Sleep, Part 2" I will give you practical ways to overcome these two forces. Instead of facing them, most people choose to go for a mind-numbing distraction, like screens. There are far better ways to work through your fear!

52. Building Healthy Sleep Habits, Part 2

As I said in part 1, reason number 3 for getting poor sleep is this: Overstimulating your brain too close to bed, with things like video games, phones, television, or your computer.

Do you find it scary to sit in silence with your own thoughts, fears, and anxieties?

Here are some solutions that have helped many athletes overcome their mental challenges and sleep like babies again:

1. *Journal for 10 minutes before bed.*

Example of a journal prompt:

   i. Write out all the lies you are telling yourself about your abilities, what people think about you, what might happen the next day, etc.
   ii. Write out all the counter truths, or what could possibly be true, about that lie you've been believing.
   iii. Read the "truths" 10 times minimum before bed.

2. Ask mom or dad to talk for 10 minutes.

I know, it's not the most fun thing in the world. But, there is no one on earth who loves you more, wants you to succeed, and will do *absolutely anything* to make sure you are mentally, emotionally, and physically healthy. Share what's on your mind and heart with them.

3. Read something positive for 10 minutes.

Grab a book on positivity, overcoming challenges, how to control your mind, how to be courageous, etc.

4. Stretch or foam roll for 10 minutes.

This will get your body right *and* your mind right! The key here is that you are keeping yourself from the temptation to be on screens or technology.

5. Pray.

If you are a person of faith, pray!

53. Active Recovery Vs. Time Off

There is a big difference between taking time off and active recovery. Time off is taking multiple days off from sports and training. Active recovery is when you are still playing sports or training, but with a much lower intensity. So many young athletes are playing on multiple teams, playing multiple sports in the same season, and going back to back seasons without any time off.

For many, "time off" means having two days of "only" skill work and running in between the championship of your football season and the tryouts of your basketball season. That is *not* time off! That is active recovery. Don't get the two confused!

RECOVERY, SLEEP, & INJURY PREVENTION

There are more young athletes than ever before who are experiencing overuse injuries and burnout. In fact, some studies show that 75% of young athletes quit sports by the age of 12.

When to Take Time Off:

1. **After intense training cycles**: If you've been training hard or playing games for weeks or months with one day off here and there at most, you would be wise to take 3 days off minimum.

2. **During illness or injury**: Unless it is the state championship or a huge, huge moment, you should take the day or week off games and practice until you are recovered from an *illness*. If it's an *injury*, listen to your body. Even if it's a big championship, pushing through an injury may become your biggest regret.

3. **Mentally Drained**: If you feel mentally drained or unmotivated, it's important to take a step back. Mental recovery is just as important as physical recovery.

When to Focus on Active Recovery

1. **During lighter training periods**: When you're not in the middle of a hard training block, active recovery allows you to stay engaged in your sport without crushing your body. It requires discipline and that is why *all* great athletes do it.

2. **Post-training**: Light exercises like walking, swimming, or stretching after a competition, game, or training session will help.

3. **After competitions**: Low-intensity activity the day after a hard run, game, or competition can actually speed up your recovery!

Sometimes your body needs time off while sometimes, active recovery is the right call. Decide once and for all that you will *listen* to your body!

54. How to Increase Flexibility, Reduce Soreness, & Recover Faster with Foam Rolling

Have you ever seen one of those long foam cylindrical things that athletes roll on? It's called a foam roller, and it is a *great* way to massage your own muscles without paying $100 for a massage.

Cost

- Foam rollers are cheap! They are between $10-$40 depending on the quality you want. A good, reliable one will cost about $20 and last for a couple years at least.

Benefits

- **Increased Flexibility and Range of Motion:** A 2017 review in the *Journal of Athletic Training* concluded that foam rolling improves flexibility, particularly when applied for 1-2 minutes per muscle group.
- **Reduced Muscle Soreness:** A 2015 study in *The Journal of Sports Medicine and Physical Fitness* found that foam rolling reduced the intensity of muscle soreness after intense exercise.
- **Quicker Muscle Recovery:** A 2014 review in *Health and Fitness Journal* concluded that foam rolling may help athletes recover faster between training sessions by increasing circulation and reducing muscle stiffness.
- **Increased Blood Flow:** A study published in the *Journal of Strength and Conditioning Research* in 2015 showed that foam rolling improved arterial function and blood flow, contributing to better muscle recovery.
- **Increased Performance:** A 2015 study in *Journal of Sports Science and Medicine* found that foam rolling combined with stretching,

when used before physical activity, improved jump performance and strength.

How you foam roll matters. When I first started foam rolling, it hurt a TON! That's actually a sign that you are doing it right.

Here is the best way to foam roll:

1. **Go Slowly.** Roll like you are ironing a shirt.
2. **One Minute Per Muscle.** Make sure to download the Free Pro Stretch and Recovery Series training videos which includes "How to Foam Roll."
3. **Stop Where It Hurts.** Pause on the areas that feel most tense, and then work to relax the muscle!
4. **Breathe!** Rolling hurts more the more you need it. Make sure to breathe!
5. **Distract Yourself.** Listen to music, watch game films, or do something else to distract yourself from the pain!

Enduringly great athletes take care of their soft tissue, which is what foam rolling does. You can learn how to foam roll alongside me by getting the Pro Stretch and Recovery Videos Series– the QR code is at the end of the next chapter.

55. Sport Specific Stretches

Every athlete knows how important stretching and being flexible is. So why do most athletes not do it?

It often hurts, it takes time, and the benefit is not always immediate. The other reason athletes push it off is because getting injured doesn't happen immediately either– it happens after days and days (and weeks and weeks) of not stretching and not taking care of your body.

> *"The pain of discipline weighs ounces, but the pain of regret weighs tons."*

Remember that quote and be wise as you begin stretching and foam rolling consistently!

Three situations when stretching is discouraged:

1. When someone has excessive movement in their joints
2. If you have recently broken a bone
3. If you have inflammation in the area (i.e. a sprain) or if you have sharp pain

Sport Specific Stretching:

While stretching is mostly dependent upon the individual and what they most need due to their tightnesses or limitations, there *are* some good stretches for specific athletes. Perform the stretches below at your own pace and desire for 1 minute each:

Examples of pec and shoulder stretches for baseball players, softball players, volleyball players, and swimmers due to overhead arm motions:

- Doorway pec stretch (90 degree bent elbow as well as 135 degree bent elbow)
- Bent over, arm overhead traction stretch (grab a hold of a partners hand, use a strap, or hold onto a stable surface in front of you, then fall back)
- Traction with rotation

RECOVERY, SLEEP, & INJURY PREVENTION

Examples of hip flexor and glute stretches for baseball players, softball players, golfers, tennis players, sprinters, and jumpers due to the need for explosive movements.

- ½ Kneeling hip flexor stretch with reach
- Pigeon pose
- 90/90 stretch

Examples of calf stretches for any athlete who runs, jumps, or cuts.

- Standing calf stretch foot against a wall
- Lying on back, towel stretch (wrap around foot, pull toe back)
- Downward facing dog

Scan the QR code or head to www.andrewjsimpson.com/everything-bonus to get the entire Pro Stretch and Recovery Series, a $37 value, at no cost. Get sport specific stretches, a follow along foam rolling video series, nutrition guidance, and more.

56. The Power of Breathing

What's the best way to calm your nerves, re-focus, relax, and let go of stress or tension? BREATHE!

You breathe 17,000 to 30,000 times a day, which means that each year, you take upwards of 11 million breaths. If you are 10 years old, that's 110 BILLION breaths.

Question for you: *how many of them have you taken with the right form?*

When you take short, shallow, "chest and shoulder" breaths, it's proven to increase your stress, tension, and even anxiety. This is definitely not helpful in pressure-packed sports situations.

When you take long, deep, "belly" breaths, it's proven to *reduce* stress, tension, and even anxiety.

Don't worry, if you haven't been taking the right kind of breaths, you have 30,000 more chances *today* to get better!

Box Breathing:

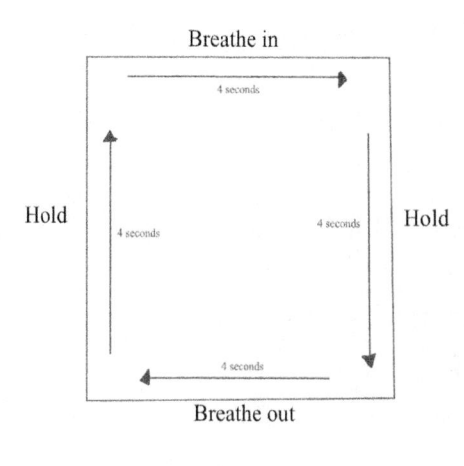

Imagine you are tracing the outline of a box. Inhale for 4 seconds as you trace across the top, hold your breath for 4 seconds as you go down the right side of the box, exhale for 4 seconds as you go across the bottom of the box, and finally hold your breath again as you go back up across the right side of the box.

RECOVERY, SLEEP, & INJURY PREVENTION

Competition Breathing When Under Pressure:

Inhale strongly for 4 seconds, and then exhale with a strong "shhhhh" sound, powerfully for 3 seconds. The "shhhhh" exhale is meant to push *out* the tense, anxious, worrisome thoughts.

Joy Breathing:

When feeling stressed or tense, inhale for 3 seconds with your eyes closed and a closed mouth smile, hold your breath for 3 seconds, and then exhale with a teeth grinning smile for 3 seconds.

"Pump You Up" Breathing:

If you are sluggish or tired before a game, workout, or competition, try this type of breathing to get you motivated. Make an "O" shape with your lips like you are about to whistle, and then exhale 10 times quickly and powerfully.

THE SIXTH
ESSENTIAL AREA OF MASTERY

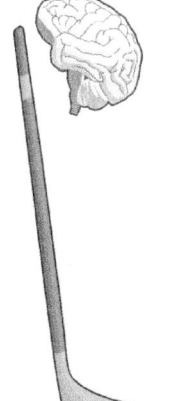

SELF LEADERSHIP, LEADING OTHERS, & STRENGTHENING RELATIONSHIPS

57. The Most Important Thing About Sports That No One Teaches You

Leading, communicating, and managing relationships is not something that comes naturally to most athletes, but it is absolutely essential if you want to win *and* enjoy your experience in sports.

This is different from being able to *"deal with people."*

A great teammate knows how to create peace and unity, seek to understand others, work together to achieve a common goal, communicate effectively, encourage and build others up, respect one another's strengths, and how to ask for help.

You are going to walk away from reading this section and immediately be able to have more influence and better relationships with your teammates, your coaches, and of course, your friends and family. Do not, under any circumstance, skip this section!

First up is learning how to do your part in creating a cohesive team.

58. Fostering Team Cohesion: The Role You Play in Creating Unity

Have you ever been part of a team where everyone was humble and shared a common goal?

This is the best kind of team to play for, and you personally play a part in building that type of culture.

Don't be the athlete who thinks, *"There is nothing I can do. My coach is _____. My teammates are _____. It's hopeless! The culture is just the way it is."*

That is a limiting belief. You *can* make a difference, but you first have to believe that you can.

When Magic Johnson came into the NBA as a rookie, the culture of his team was too serious, no fun at all, and everyone was scared to show enthusiasm or too much positivity for fear of being judged by the veteran players. Magic didn't care. He knew that if the team had more fun together and was more positive, they could be capable of even more!

Kareem Abdul Jabaar, a hall of famer, didn't like Magic Johnson's high energy and enthusiasm, and would ridicule Magic when he started to show too much positivity.

Magic stood strong, believing that this *was* an important thing for the culture and that he *could* make a difference.

By the end of the season, the Lakers were crushing competitors and *every player*, including Kareem, was acting more like Magic.

Belief that you can, and the decision that you *will*, make a positive impact on your team's culture is the first and most important secret to creating a unified team. Remember this!

59. The #1 Threat to Team Harmony—and How You Can Stop It

I have some important questions for you:

1. How many shots should a player take and miss before they stop shooting?
2. When does *confidence* actually become *cockiness*? When do you consider a person a ball hog? After how many shots?

3. How should a player communicate to his or her teammates on the field? Should they signal with their hands one time? Should they yell? Should they run over to their teammate when the ball is dead?

4. How many errors should a player be allowed to make before the coach benches them?

5. What does a good teammate do? What does it mean to be a bad teammate?

6. What does working hard in the gym look like? What does it look like for a person to slack off?

7. What should a player do after they mess up? Should they apologize to the team? Should they stay positive and smile? Should they get mad?

8. How many times should a teammate ask you to come practice with them if you keep saying no? 2 times? 3 times?

I bet my answers to those questions are slightly, if not significantly, different from yours. And I bet your and your teammates' answers are different as well.

Why? Because we all see the world differently.

What's my point?

The #1 thing that destroys team unity and culture is *expectations*. When a team is filled with individuals who expect that everyone else should think more like *them* and be more like *them*, the outcome is a terrible team culture.

The beautiful part of being on a team is the *differences* that people bring to the table.

SELF LEADERSHIP, LEADING OTHERS, & STRENGTHENING RELATIONSHIPS

Winning teams are filled with individuals who:

- Work hard to understand the way their teammates think and act
- Respect and learn to appreciate others for who they are
- Strive to connect and build relationships with their teammates, *especially* the ones who are different from you
- Communicate with clarity, honesty, and vulnerability when there are disagreements or arguments
- Refuse to participate in gossip

We are going to cover all of this and more in the following chapters!

60. How to Win the Trust and Respect of Your Teammates

One of the most important ingredients for a championship team and championship culture is *trust*.

Here are a few really, really, really important things you need to know and do if you want to be trusted and respected by your teammates:

1. **Be the MCE:** The Most Consistent Encourager. When your teammates are doing something well, high five them and verbally let them know. When your teammates are playing poorly, be the first one to encourage them and let them know you believe in them. This is *particularly* important when the game is on the line, when your emotions are saying "get mad at that person", or any other time where you do not *feel* like being there to lift them up.

2. **Be the HWP:** The Hardest Worker PERIOD. It's not about being harder working than your teammates, it's about working as hard

as *you* possibly can. If you want to be respected by your teammates, especially older and more experienced teammates, put in the work. Master your position, improve your skills, and be the best you can be.

3. **Be a CCC:** A Clear and Consistent Communicator. When you are unclear about an expectation your coach or teammate has for you, ask for clarification. *"I'm sorry John, I want to make sure I understand. When Sam cuts, am I supposed to go to the left, or right?"* When you are frustrated that the team isn't performing well, clearly communicate your frustrations in a calm, solution oriented manner. Ask for help, ask for clarification, and communicate your thoughts, ideas, and feelings in a productive way. Be a great two-way communicator!

4. **Be a BIC:** A Beast In the Classroom. You are a student-athlete. Student first, athlete second. Never give your coach or teammates a reason to lose trust in you because you failed to take care of your assignments and studies. If you end up getting benched or not being able to suit up due to poor grades or behavior in school, you will surely lose respect from your teammates!

5. **Be a GNT:** A Giver Not a Taker. Be the kind of teammate who walks into the room and asks, "How can I help?" rather than "What's in it for me?" If you start to think it's all about you, your team will start to resent you. Offer a helping hand, share your ideas, and strive to contribute *wherever the team needs you,* even if it's not your favorite position! Help the team win and the team will help you. Give first!

61. Improve Your Relationship With Coaches and Older Teammates

Coming off of the last point, "being a giver not a taker," it's important for every athlete to learn how to influence the people "above them." This mainly means your coaches and older teammates.

The athletes who end up having the best sports career are the ones who master the art of *leading up* (that is, leading people who are older than you) without *sucking up*.

Credit goes to John Maxwell, author of the 360 Leader, for the following concepts that I also write about in my book *ATHLETE! I'm Talking To You.*

#1 Lead yourself incredibly well.

Do everything in your power to work hard, be consistent, be the most positive person on your team, practice good habits, and do the things you don't feel like doing.

#2 Lighten your coach's load, as well as the older players on the team.

Every coach has problems. Every coach has a list of 95 things they need to do throughout the week. What can you take off his or her plate? How can you better support your coach? Write down all of your ideas now!

#3 Be willing to do what others won't.

Few things will gain the appreciation of your coaches more quickly than a player with a do-whatever-it-takes attitude. What are the things that everyone on the team avoids doing? Do those things to the best of your ability.

EVERYTHING YOUNG ATHLETES SHOULD KNOW

#4 Come prepared every time you have one-on-one time with your coach.

Don't just expect your coach to do all the talking. Ask your coach to meet every once in a while and do a few things to prepare:

1. Bring ideas on what you think you can do to help the team be better.
2. Thank your coach for something specific that you appreciate about them. Coaching is not an easy job!
3. Ask your coach what he or she needs from you. Where does the coach want you to step up? Ask them!

If you do those four things above, you will gain even more respect from the team. This is all about having a serve-first mindset. It's all about going the extra mile to help your coach and teammates. Could you imagine if *everyone* on the team did this?

62. How to Be a Leader to Your Teammates Who Are Peers

Do you ever feel awkward or strange trying to lead your teammates who are the same age as you?

Is there a part of you that feels like when you do this, you are acting like you are better than them? Even though you don't believe that, it can feel like it.

I want to share with you the 5 principles of leading your peers that will help you while helping them, as well:

1. **Aim to complete your teammates, not compete with them.** A teammate can smell you trying to beat them from a mile away. Don't aim to be better than them, aim to be better than you were yesterday.

SELF LEADERSHIP, LEADING OTHERS, & STRENGTHENING RELATIONSHIPS

2. **Be a good friend.** Before you can influence your teammates, you must first build a relationship with them. Get to know the real them by asking questions about their likes and dislikes, their goals and challenges, and showing authentic interest in what they share with you.

3. **Avoid gossip and complaining.** Before you can effectively lead your fellow teammates, you must earn their respect by being a person who is *above* gossip and complaining.

4. **Ask for their advice.** Even if you think you have the answer, by asking for your fellow teammates input or advice, you elevate them and win their trust.

5. **Don't pretend you're perfect.** Since nobody is perfect – not you, not your teammates, not your coach – we need to quit pretending. People who are real and genuine regarding their weaknesses as well as their strengths will gain influence with their teammates.

Pretending we are perfect doesn't get us anywhere. Instead, admitting faults, asking for advice, worrying less about what others think, being open to learning from others, and putting away pride and pretense are important steps to help us move in the right direction and win over those around us.

63. How to Lead Your Younger, Less Experienced Teammates

Leading younger players should be the easiest thing to do, but oftentimes it becomes the hardest to execute. Do you ever find yourself getting annoyed, impatient, or frustrated with the younger people on the team?

> ➤ They take too long to learn things.
> ➤ They aren't as mature as you.

EVERYTHING YOUNG ATHLETES SHOULD KNOW

- They aren't as committed.
- They aren't as skilled.

I understand all of these things. But hey, *that's why they need you!*

Here are the 8 keys to being the leader you always wish you had:

1. **See everyone as a "10."** If you see a person as they are, they will stay where they are. If you see them as they could be, they will become all they *can* be.

2. **Model the behavior you want to see in them.** If you want a team culture of kindness and inclusion, be kind to them and include them. If you want a team culture of hard work and focus, be that type of player all the time. Don't be a hypocrite!

3. **Be available.** Being too busy for your teammates is not cool. Make sure the younger players know you are always available to help them get better or work through challenges.

4. **Be the CEO: Chief Encouragement Officer.** Younger players are always second guessing themselves and are often insecure. Give 4 compliments for every 1 criticism.

5. **Encourage Failure and Don't Overreact.** Don't freak out and overreact when a younger player messes up. Instead ask, "What did you learn? How would you do it differently next time?"

6. **Ask for their opinion.** Man this one will feel good. "They actually care about my opinion!" Do this one *often*.

7. **Invite them to workout.** Self explanatory. Go out of our way to include them!

8. **Connect outside of practice.** Be relational: invite them to get lunch, hang out, or practice together!

SELF LEADERSHIP, LEADING OTHERS, & STRENGTHENING RELATIONSHIPS

The highest level of leadership is developing other leaders. This is an honor; take it seriously and implement these 8 tips above!

64. How to Have "Difficult" Conversations and Confront People Without Making Them Feel *Less* Than You

Step 1: ~~Difficult Conversations~~ → Meaningful, Helpful Conversations

Your words matter. If you constantly refer to these types of conversations with people as "hard" or "difficult," then you will resist them. The truth is that these types of conversations are the most *meaningful* and *transformational* conversations you can have with another person!

I want you to think about the last time you were upset with a teammate or coach, you disagreed with them, or you really *wanted* to say something to them. But, you didn't. You rationalized with yourself, *"It's not worth my time."*

Maybe it wasn't, maybe it was. The point is that you had an opportunity to be courageous and *strengthen* your team culture and relationship with that person. But you missed it.

Consistently after you have one of these conversations, you will realize a few things:

1. It wasn't as bad as you thought it was going to be. In your mind, you played it out like it was going to be 10x worse than it was. But the reality is that *they* were pretty nervous too and just wanted to clear the air.

2. You didn't know what they were really feeling. Having the conversation helped you to see things from their point of view, which helped your perspective.

3. It feels bad before, OK during, and really, really, really good after the conversation. Remember this next time you go into it. You *will* feel so much better afterwards.

Final Tips for Meaningful Conversations:

1. **Have the conversation quickly.** Set up a time to talk to the person as soon as possible.
2. **Seek first to understand their side of things.** Ask questions. "What are you feeling after that situation that happened yesterday? What's going through your mind?"
3. **Tell them how you are feeling, not what you think is wrong with them.** "You did this, you did that." Instead start with, "I'm sure this wasn't your intention, but I am feeling upset and am lacking confidence after you called me out at practice yesterday for taking a bad shot."

65. What To Do When Teammates Don't Care As Much As You Do

Have you ever done a project in school where no one really cared and it was all left to *you* to make it great?

How did that feel? Did it really anger you, but you said "Whatever, I don't care," and tried to brush it off?

Not everyone is going to care as much as you, but there are 3 things you can do to help your own mindset during those times and to actually get them to care more.

1. **Trade your expectations for appreciation.** We talked about this earlier, but it's true here as well. Instead of expecting everyone to

"do their fair share," you should go into it expecting to do all the work (which means you also gain all the experience) and be *excited* if someone ends up stepping up and doing anything. Then you will appreciate them more when they do contribute.

2. **Ask better questions, have a better mindset.** Is it annoying? Is it unfortunate? Or, is this an opportunity to grow and get better? What *could* be great about this if you really had to find something great about this? An athlete who learns to ask themselves better questions is an athlete who has just discovered the secret to replacing breakdowns with breakthroughs.

3. **Be honest and ask for their help.** One by one, talk to your teammates individually and let them know that you are struggling and feeling like there is a lot of pressure on you. Ask for their help instead of telling them they are wrong or that they don't work hard enough. Can you see how they might receive this better?

You cannot change people, but you can influence them by always being kind and respectful. Simply put, if your teammates do not care as much as you, you have 3 choices:

1. **Get over it:** Continue to work as hard and smart as you possibly can. Put your focus where it counts most.

2. **Change your mindset:** Look for the benefits. "I get more reps in. It's an opportunity to lead."

3. **Work to influence them:** Build a relationship with them, invite them to workout with you, and help them. It will take time, but it will be worth it.

You are a leader. Whether you like it or not, you are a leader. Your job is to lead!

Which of the 3 choices above are you going to make today to better handle teammates who are not as committed as you?

66. What To Do If You Are Feeling Pressure From Parents

Do you feel pressure from your parents to do well in sports? Do you feel like they are too involved?

More importantly, do *they* know how you feel?

I have talked to many, many parents who had *no clue* that their athlete was feeling the way they are feeling.

It is *your* responsibility to yourself, your family, and your teammates to talk to your parents about how you are feeling.

> "Hey Dad, I am sure you don't realize this, but I just want to let you know I am feeling a lot of pressure from you to perform well and it's negatively affecting my performance."

> "Hey Mom, can we talk? Before games when you talk to me about the game and give me reminders, it adds stress to me. I know you are just trying to help, but can you stop doing that?"

Athlete, you are strong. You are brave. You are capable of having these meaningful conversations.

Have them quickly and remember, it's going to be better after you do.

But if you avoid it, the problem will grow.

Big problems were once small problems that went unaddressed for way too long.

Your mom and dad want what's best for you. If you help them to understand what you are feeling, it's going to make them happier, not mad.

THE SEVENTH
ESSENTIAL AREA OF MASTERY

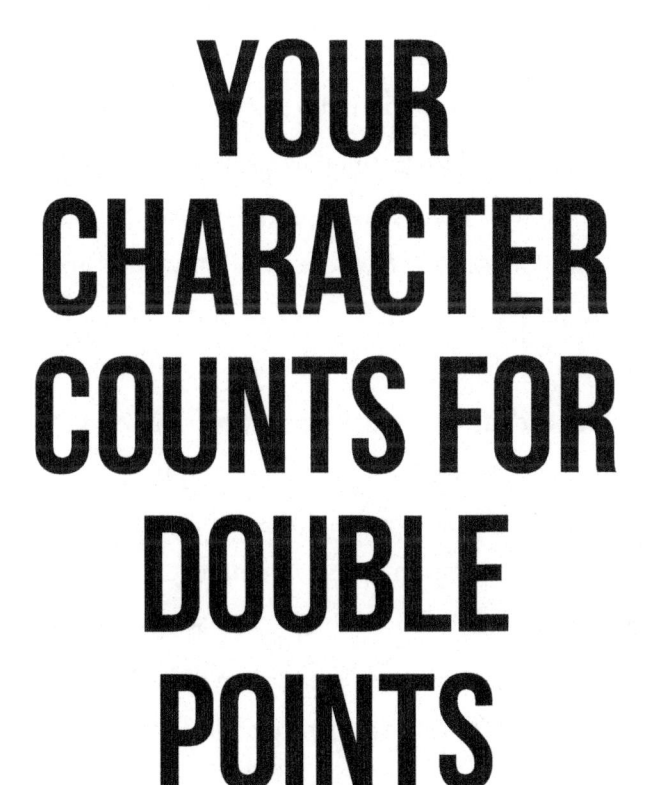

YOUR CHARACTER COUNTS FOR DOUBLE POINTS

67. Humility

One of the top character qualities that the best coaches and teams look for in players is *humility*. That's why I am putting it first! Humility is so much more than "not being cocky." Just because you are not cocky does *not* mean you are humble.

Humble players do a few things differently from non-humble players:

1. **They don't get defensive when they receive feedback.** Have you ever received negative feedback from a coach and immediately felt like you were "less than?" This is a mindset thing. Feedback is the breakfast of champions. Don't get defensive, get *curious*. "How can I use what I just received to make myself and the team better?"

2. **They ask for feedback, they don't just tolerate it.** Good players accept feedback, great players crave it. Ask your coach to critique the areas of your game where you know you are weak. Half of fame basketball player Tim Duncan once said, "Good, better, best. Never let it rest. 'Til your good is better and your better is best."

3. **They do the dirty work, no matter their age or stage.** For humble players, the more they accomplish, the lower they go. Humble players volunteer to do the "dirty work." They don't have a "freshman pick up the trash" mentality. Instead, they continue to mop the floor, carry the water, and serve the team.

4. **They talk to everyone and treat everyone like a "10."** Remember this one from "leading younger players?" Humble players do not think too highly of themselves, even if they are the best. They walk into practice or into the locker room and say "There you are!" instead of "Here I am!" For them it's "look at you" instead of "look at me."

YOUR CHARACTER COUNTS FOR DOUBLE POINTS

5. **They play for the name on the front of the jersey.** Humble players are constantly asking, "what do I need to do to help the team win?" They play for the name on the front of the jersey, not for the name on the back. If they need to change positions or come off the bench, they do it!

Humility: write it down on a piece of paper and put on your mirror. Write it in your glove, your hat, or practice jersey. Add it as an alarm clock label on your phone and have it go off at 7 am, 12 noon, and 4 pm. Check your ego at the door and remember that "humility" is one of the most attractive, if not *the most* attractive, qualities to a coach!

68. GRIT

Angela Duckworth, author of the book "GRIT", defines grit as a combination of **passion** and **perseverance** for long-term goals.

In her research, she emphasizes that grit *is* about working hard, but it is also about maintaining focus and effort over time, especially when faced with challenges or setbacks.

How do you rate yourself with GRIT on a scale of 1-10? _____

Kobe Bryant's Grit

Kobe Bryant's journey to becoming one of the best basketball players of all time was all about grit—passion and hard work.

When he joined the NBA at 17, many people doubted him. Early on, he struggled and faced criticism, especially after missing big shots. Instead of quitting, Kobe worked harder than anyone. He practiced for hours, arriving before the sun came up and staying long after practice ended.

EVERYTHING YOUNG ATHLETES SHOULD KNOW

His "Mamba Mentality" meant always pushing through, even when things were tough. Despite injuries, like when he tore his achilles tendon, he never stopped trying to improve. Over 20 years, Kobe won five NBA championships and became one of the best players to ever play the game. His story shows that talent alone isn't enough—grit is necessary if you are going to become the best you can be.

Starting today you can become a "grittier" player.

Decide right now that:

1. I am in this for the long haul. Temporary setbacks, injuries, or failures will not derail my focus! _____ Enter Your Initials Here

2. I will work hard today, tomorrow, and every single day whether I feel like it, or not. _____ Enter Your Initials Here

3. Challenges are for champions. When faced with one, I will look at it as an opportunity to grow. Whether the coach benches me, I miss a game winning shot, or I swim the worst race of my life, I will look for ways to grow and get better. _____ Enter Your Initials Here

Remember, hard work beats talent when talent doesn't work hard!

69. Discipline

John Wooden, the greatest basketball coach of all time, defined discipline as the ability to do what you know you should do, when you should do it, whether you feel like it or not.

"Coach" as they called him, emphasized that discipline is a key to success, especially when it comes to making consistent, smart decisions and putting in the effort even when motivation might not be there.

YOUR CHARACTER COUNTS FOR DOUBLE POINTS

Do you wait for motivation, or create motivation?

Take a moment to list out all of the things you know you should do if you want to reach your goals. This could be running, skill work, eating healthy, going to bed on time, etc.

My List of Successful Actions and Habits:

- ➤ _____
- ➤ _____
- ➤ _____
- ➤ _____
- ➤ _____
- ➤ _____

Serena Williams is an example of a pro athlete who achieved huge success with discipline. She was naturally talented but that alone was not the key to her greatness.

As a young athlete, she was all about hard work. While other kids were hanging out, she was on the court, practicing with her sister Venus and sticking to a strict routine. As she achieved more and more, Serena never stopped pushing herself. She trained hard, ate right, and stayed mentally tough, no matter what. Even when injuries hit, she stayed disciplined and focused on getting back to her best.

Her commitment paid off with 23 Grand Slam singles titles, the most by any player in the era. Serena's story is a powerful reminder: Talent gets you noticed, but discipline gets you to the top ranks in your sport!

70. Responsibility and Taking Ownership

Responsibility = response-ability → your ability to respond.

How do you respond when your team loses?

How do you respond when you miss the shot, drop the ball, or don't perform up to the standard?

Do you take ownership for your mistakes, or do you make excuses?

I know that my natural tendency is to make excuses. Why? Because I do *not* want other people thinking that I am not good enough, that I am a slacker, or that I forgot something.

My identity is that I want to be seen and known as a committed, talented, smart, high performing player.

And, if anything interferes with that, I get defensive.

Bill Belichick was the head coach of the New England Patriots and won a whopping 6 Super Bowls during that time. Responsibility was a key element of their greatness.

His famous motto, *"Do your job,"* isn't just about what happens on the field; it's about taking ownership of your actions and putting the team first.

Coach Bill believes that if every player focuses on their individual responsibility, the whole team will work together and succeed. I tend to agree.

He says, *"Accountability is a huge part of what we do, both individually and as a group."*

Responsibility means showing up, working hard, and trusting that your teammates are doing the same. It's a lesson for you and I both- success doesn't happen unless everyone takes responsibility for their part!

Writing exercise: How do I respond when things do not go my way?

_____

_____

_____

_____

How would the best version of me respond? How would my role models respond?

_____

_____

_____

_____

71. Long-Range Patience, Part 1

Have you ever had the experience where someone next to you is tapping their pencil repeatedly on the table and it begins to drive you nuts?

Or, when your younger sibling keeps poking and hitting you? Or, someone nearby is yelling when you are trying to talk to someone?

These things cause you to lose your short term patience at times, but this is not the kind of patience I am referring to when it comes to developing your character as an athlete.

Long-term patience is the X-factor of champion athletes.

I know an athlete named Sarah who is a 14 year old lacrosse player. She had just finished up a great season where she started every game.

During her first session at our personal training gym she said to me, "I just feel like I should be so much further along. Sure I started every game, but I only scored 12 goals during the fall season."

"When did you start playing lacrosse?" I asked her.

"Last spring" she said.

My response: "What!? Let me get this straight. The fall season was only your second season ever playing lacrosse and you started every game and scored 12 goals!?"

This helped us have a great conversation around patience and persistence.

You cannot expect to work hard at something for 3 months, a year, or even 3 years and expect to be the best. It takes time.

It reminds me of the bamboo tree. Have you ever heard the story?

72. Long-Range Patience, Part 2: The Bamboo Tree

The Chinese bamboo tree is one of the strongest, most durable, most impressive plants in existence.

The versatility of this plant is endless. Its power is significant.

But how does the strongest plant in the world become the strongest? *Patience.*

YOUR CHARACTER COUNTS FOR DOUBLE POINTS

It begins life as a large, hard seed the size of a softball. The gardener takes that seed, buries it deep into the ground, and begins watering and caring for it day after day.

After 3 months, there is no sign of growth. Ugh! 3 months of work and you see *no results*? That's frustrating.

Ok, the gardener keeps watering and taking care of this seed day after day, never missing a day. The gardener knows if the seed misses one day of water, it's likely to die. Then the whole process would start over.

After 1 year of watering and caring for the plant, *nothing*. But what about after 2 years? Surely there is some visible progress! Maybe a little bud sprouting out of the ground? *No, nothing.*

3 years? *Still nothing.*

After 5 years, something remarkable begins to occur. Over the next 6 weeks, the Chinese bamboo tree shoots up more than 90 feet! It's incredible. You can actually see it growing if you sit and look at it for a while!

90 feet in 6 weeks. *90 feet in 6 weeks.* 90 feet is 10 times taller than the ceilings in the majority of houses.

Critical Question: did the tree *really* grow 90 feet in 6 weeks?

Of course it didn't. It grew 90 feet in 5 years and 6 weeks.

That's how growth occurs. My friend, if you are not *yet* seeing the results you truly desire, and you are doing the right things, *keep going*. It is guaranteed that if you keep doing the right things, for long enough, you will eventually achieve Chinese bamboo tree-type growth!

EVERYTHING YOUNG ATHLETES SHOULD KNOW

73. Integrity

Kerry Wood is a former Major League Baseball pitcher who played for the Cubs.

In his own words, Wood has said about integrity:

> "Integrity is doing the right thing when no one is looking. It's about doing what you say you're going to do, holding yourself to a high standard, and being accountable to yourself and others."

How are you doing with your integrity?

When you say you are going to go out and go for a run, do you do it?

When no one is watching, how do you warm up? Do you stretch?

When you tell your coach that you are going to study game film, do you do it?

When no one is watching, what are you eating?

You do not have to be perfect to have integrity, but you have to have integrity to be the leader and athlete you are capable of becoming!

Steph Curry, future hall of fame basketball player known for his incredible skills and performance *as well as* his character off the court said this about integrity: "Integrity is doing the right thing when no one's watching. It's about treating people right, being a good teammate, and being the best version of yourself, no matter what."

Russell Wilson, future hall of fame quarterback, gave a similar definition of integrity: "Integrity is doing the right thing, even when no one is looking.

It's about being honest with yourself, staying true to your values, and always doing what's best for your team and your family. Integrity is everything."

Whether it's Kerry Wood, Steph Curry, or Russell Wilson, there appears to be a common theme when it comes to integrity: *Doing the right thing, what is best for your teammates and family, when no one is looking.*

Assess yourself honestly and live with extreme integrity today. It *will* pay off!

74. Enthusiasm

"I'm not really the outgoing type."

"I prefer to stay quiet."

No problem. You can still be enthusiastic! In fact, you have a responsibility to your team and your future self to be enthusiastic.

If you are not excited or enthusiastic about practice or games or weight room workouts, it's nearly impossible to perform to your ultimate potential.

How do you become more enthusiastic?

1. Think about the end goal or benefit of what you are doing.

Even if you don't love working out, you can learn to love the *results* that are going to come! Imagine being able to sprint into the paint, the crease, or the heart of the defense in any sport and be able to stand your ground. Nothing can knock you down, you are unstoppable!

Imagine standing on the podium receiving a gold medal. Can you get enthusiastic about that? Before practices and before training especially, you must show up with enthusiasm. And one way to do so is to *visualize the end goal you desire!*

2. Think about your team.

Maybe you are saying to yourself, "That's for the older guys or girls on the team. The seniors, the captains. They should be like that. But me? I'm young, I need to stay calm."

Remember Magic Johnson? He was a rookie when he showed up and inspired his entire championship team to have more enthusiasm!

Everyone wants to play on a team where there is excitement and people show up each day eager to work toward winning. If that does not exist on your team, who is going to bring it? *You are, I hope!*

3. "I AM" Enthusiastic.

Everyday, say it out loud. Say it until you feel it, believe it, and become it!

75. Poise

Earlier in chapter 6 we talked about pressure. Pressure has the power to disrupt your *poise* if you let it. There are few things you can begin doing today to have more poise under pressure:

1. **Prepare.** When you go to take a test in school, are you more calm when you have studied extensively *or* when you haven't studied at all? Preparation creates poise. Michael Jordan, arguably the greatest basketball player of all time, said it this way: "The key to success is confidence. And the key to confidence is preparation. When the game is on the line, if you've put in the work and the preparation, it's just another opportunity to show what you've got."

2. **Visualize Yourself.** If you cannot see it you cannot be it. Close your eyes right now and see yourself remaining calm and poised in pressure packed situations. Visualize yourself taking deep breaths, smiling, and standing tall with confidence.

3. **Visualize Your Role Model.** If you have trouble seeing yourself poised, instead visualize yourself as your favorite pro athlete. Pick an athlete who is calm under pressure, and see yourself as them. Walk, talk, move, and perform the way they do as you visualize the play.

4. **Be an Animal.** Not literally, but mentally, imagine yourself as your favorite animal that you believe is the calmest, most poised of all the animals. Is it a lion? An eagle? Many athletes have done this before and it can really help with your mental state during a game.

5. **Use Your Breath and Body.** Slow external movements create calmness internally. Slow, deep breaths create poise. If you are fidgety, pacing, talking and moving frequently, it's going to be hard to have poise.

6. **Normalize Failure.** Champion tennis player Maria Sharapova has said: "Pressure is part of the game. The important thing is how you react to it. I always try to remind myself to breathe, stay calm, and believe in my game. Once you're able to do that, the pressure doesn't seem so bad."

The sooner you accept that you will not be perfect and that every mistake, loss, or bad performance is a *stepping stone to success*, you will find yourself more poised under pressure!

76. Don't Cut Corners, Do the Work and Do it Well

Industriousness is a word that you don't see very often. It's another John Wooden special. I didn't mention it before, but Coach Wooden led his

EVERYTHING YOUNG ATHLETES SHOULD KNOW

UCLA Bruins basketball team to 10 National Championships, 7 of them being consecutive wins. Yes, 7 Division One College Basketball National Championships IN A ROW!

How did he do it? One way was by helping his players develop the character quality of *industriousness*.

Would you describe your work ethic and the way you approach practices as industrious?

Industriousness is the quality of being hard-working and putting in the effort without cutting corners.

If you want to be all that you are capable of becoming, which I believe is a lot, then you've got to show up every day, do the little things right, and never, ever, ever cut corners.

I remember when I played football in high school and we would run laps, I literally would cut the corners of the field to shorten how far I had to run. No wonder why I didn't accomplish my goals in football!

Instead of eating healthy and getting adequate rest, some athletes drink energy drinks. Cutting corners.

Instead of watching game film and studying the opponent, some athletes choose to skip that boring stuff and go have fun. Cutting corners.

Instead of mastering the fundamentals, some athletes try to skip right to the complex, fancy movements in their sport. Cutting corners.

Instead of stretching and recovery by icing the knees, some athletes think they can ignore the element of recovery and just do the fun skill work. Cutting corners.

YOUR CHARACTER COUNTS FOR DOUBLE POINTS

Industriousness means doing the little things with excellence when no one is watching. That way, when someone is watching, they can tell you've been working.

Writing exercise: Where have you been cutting corners? What will you do today to become more industrious?

_____

_____

_____

_____

Don't cut corners. Do the work, and do it well!

77. Self Control

Tiger Woods, one of the greatest golfers of all time, had this to say about self-control- "I've had a lot of injuries, and I've had to learn how to be patient, how to allow my body time to heal. That requires a lot of self-discipline, because you just want to get back out there."

Patience when coming back from an injury is just one of the ways an athlete needs to exhibit self control.

A research study from the Journal of Applied Physiology* studied 639 players from top Premier leagues, as well as second-tier soccer leagues. The study concluded that soccer players with better self-control tend to have healthier routines and more practice time, leading to improved performance.

Having the self discipline to control your focus and practice time is yet another example of how an athlete can exhibit self control.

The final example is controlling your emotions. You miss a wide open shot. The opponent knocks you down illegally and the ref doesn't see it. Your teammate is ball hogging.

Things are not going your way. What do you do? Keep your emotions in check and under control! How?

Act medium. Use your Mindset Reset Tool. Revisit section one of this book!

Self control is not a nice to have, it's a must. Mick Fanning, Usain Bolt, Roger Federer. These are a few top tier athletes who were known for keeping their cool no matter the circumstances.

One reason athletes lose control of their emotions is because too much of their worth and identity is in their sport. Let me explain in the next chapter.

> *__Citation:__ Toering, T., & Jordet, G. (2015). Self-Control in Professional Soccer Players. Journal of Applied Sport Psychology, 27(3), 335–350. https://doi.org/10.1080/10413200.2015.1010047

78. Self Worth

Where do you find your sense of worthiness?

Is it in the amount of goals or points you score? Is it in the amount of playing time you get? Does it depend on whether or not your coach pays attention to you or gives you compliments?

The easiest way to tell where you draw your sense of worth from is by observing your actions and emotions when things do not go as planned.

YOUR CHARACTER COUNTS FOR DOUBLE POINTS

The more of your worth that you place in something, the more emotion you get about it and the longer those emotions last.

At the time of me writing this, Scottie Scheffler is the #1 ranked golfer in the world and has been for the last 84 weeks in a row. That's some extraordinary success.

When asked about the importance of golf in his life, here is what he said: *"Golf is something I love doing, but I always remind myself that there's more to life than golf. At the end of the day, my faith and my relationships are what matter most."*

Did you catch that? Golf is, at best, the third priority in his life. This is why he is so relaxed and calm in the most pressure packed situations!

"I try not to place too much of my identity in what I do out here on the golf course," he said in a recent press conference. *"There's a whole other part of my life that is not in front of you guys that I think is what's most important to me.*

"So, yeah, my life's not a golf score, it's not how many trophies I'm going to win, it's not anything like that. I'm proud to have a great wife (Meredith) and a great family, and we have great friends at home and I'm very grateful for the other part of my life that's away from the golf course."

Whether you are 10, 15, or 20 years old, this might be the most important thing you get out of this book. Why?

Because like Inky Johnson, my friend and athlete Carly Heine, or the once dual sport pro athlete Bo Jackson, sports can be gone in the blink of an eye. *Who you are* will outlast your sport. Remember, sports are what you do, they are not who you are!

79. Competitive Spirit

Defined as a person's drive, enthusiasm, and determination to succeed and excel in a competitive environment, competitive spirit is an essential quality for you to develop as an athlete.

It's kind of like being *hungry and under control*. Why?

Because sportsmanship is a part of having a competitive spirit. Competition was created to make us better, not bitter. To make us grow, not crush another person's growth.

It's about competing hard, with the absolute fullness of your heart and soul, while respecting your opponents and the rules of the game. A competitive player who does not respect others has no business playing the game!

Enjoy the 4 stories below, some of the greatest comebacks in sports history:

1. The Miracle at Medinah

In 2012, the European Ryder Cup team faced a huge challenge. They were down 6-10 to the U.S. and needed 8 1/2 points on the final day. But the Europeans didn't give up. They built momentum early and ended with a jaw-dropping performance, highlighted by Martin Kaymer's clutch 8-footer to seal the win.

2. The Pats 2017 Super Bowl Comeback

Down 28-3 to the Falcons, the Patriots seemed finished in Super Bowl LI. But Tom Brady never quit. He led an epic 25-point rally, tying the game with minutes to spare. The Patriots won in overtime, marking the largest comeback in Super Bowl history.

3. Liverpool's Miracle in Istanbul

At halftime, Liverpool's Champions League final against AC Milan seemed over—down 3-0. But in just seven minutes after the break, they pulled off one of the most incredible comebacks in sports, scoring three goals to tie the game. They went on to win in a shootout!

4. The Cubs' 2016 World Series Comeback

Facing a 3-1 deficit in the 2016 World Series, the Chicago Cubs were on the brink of heartbreak. But they didn't quit. They won three straight games, including a thrilling Game 7, to clinch their first championship in 108 years.

Compete until that final whistle blows and remember to never, ever, ever, EVER give up!

80. Aggressiveness

It's time to flip the switch and crank it up to 212 degrees.

212? What's that all about? At 211 degrees, water is just hot. It does *nothing*. At 212 degrees, just *one degree more,* water boils. Boiling water produces steam, and steam is enough to power a locomotion!

That is how aggressiveness works. You are playing your sport, going through the motions, and perhaps playing well. And then, all the sudden, you turn it up just one degree. You flip that switch and are now playing at a level above the rest of the competition.

Aggression, kind of like competitive spirit, is a differentiator between good and great athletes. But it must be coupled with *self control.* How aggressive are you? Has a coach or parent ever told you that you need to be more aggressive?

By this point of the book we have talked about a lot. We discussed *fear* extensively, which is something that holds athletes back from being aggressive. Many athletes hold back and play passively due to fear.

EVERYTHING YOUNG ATHLETES SHOULD KNOW

I want you to think about this real quick: *If you do not choose to flip the switch and become more aggressive, you should be scared of the potential outcomes, such as:*

The football player who does not run full speed ahead to make a tackle will end up getting hurt by the running back who runs them over.

The softball player that does not attack the ground ball will likely ride the bench.

The lacrosse player that does not attack the crease full speed will get knocked over and miss an opportunity to score.

The golfer who is not aggressive attacking the pin when down by a stroke on the final hole leaves room for the other player to sneak in and beat them.

Of course, you need to have a solid sports IQ to know when it's time to be aggressive and when it's time to pull back.

The key is to make sure that the four letter word called F-E-A-R is never the reason for a lack of aggression.

THE EIGHTH
ESERNTIAL AREA OF MASTERY

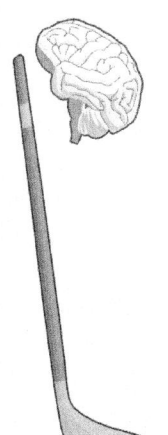

WINNING THE RECRUITING GAME

+

EVERYTHING YOU SHOULD KNOW ABOUT PLAYING COLLEGE SPORTS

81. Overview: Recruiting and the College Sports Landscape

You thought sports were the only game you played—until college recruiting entered the conversation.

The recruiting process is its own game, and if you don't know how to play, you could miss out on the opportunities you've worked so hard to create.

The reality is that many student-athletes and families waste valuable time and money chasing recruiting efforts that don't produce results. Others underestimate their potential and fail to take the critical steps necessary to stand out in a highly competitive process.

This section is designed to change that. I'm excited to introduce Christopher Stack, aka "Coach Stack," an expert in college sports recruiting. Christopher is the author of "Own Your College Recruiting Process," and the founder of Guiding Future Stars, an organization dedicated to educate and prepare student-athletes and their families to navigate the complexities of the college recruiting process and beyond.

Coach Stack is about to lay out a clear path to help you take control of your recruiting journey—from defining your vision and building your brand, to gaining exposure and being seen.

If you're a middle school or underclassman athlete, this section is a must-read to prepare for what lies ahead. If you're a senior, it's the playbook you need right now to maximize your opportunities.

Now, before we get to Coach Stack's top 5 lessons, let's look at the 7 costly mistakes athletes make that waste time, energy, and money.

82. 7 Costly Mistakes Parents and Coaches Make During the Recruiting Process

My goal in this section is to help you achieve the college sports career of your dreams. The best way to achieve that goal is to tell you in advance the 7 most common, costly mistakes that many parents and athletes make in the recruiting journey.

Here are those 7 mistakes:

1. **Lack of an exposure plan.** You need to create an online presence to compete with all of the other athletes in the recruiting space.
2. **Relying on luck.** "If I am good enough, they will find me." Yes, but the results better be so extraordinary that you are 10x ahead of any athlete in your county and possibly even region!
3. **Relying too heavily on your travel or club team to get you noticed.** You need to have many irons in the fire - your club team is just one of them.
4. **Having a "go big or go home" mindset.** Some athletes have their mind set on a huge D1 school. Keep that as a goal, but remain open minded!
5. **Waiting too long to begin the process.** The sooner you can start, the better!
6. **Not following up with the coaches.** Coaches are busy. It's up to you to stay on their radar!
7. **Not looking for schools that are recruiting your specific position.** If you are a great catcher but your desired school already has 4 catchers, it doesn't mean it's a "no," but it's not the ideal situation for you. Be open-minded!

Now, let's dive deeper into what you need to do to avoid making those mistakes and set yourself up for success.

I encourage you to reach out to Coach Stack with Guiding Future Stars or another recruiting specialist to learn more about the up-to-date rules and regulations of recruiting.

It's *always* changing. With NIL (name, image, and likeness) and other new ways for college athletes to make money, you will want to do your homework and get educated.

We've included a special resource with the bonuses that come with the book called **8 Recruiting Resources to Save You Time & Money.**

Scan the QR code to grab those, no cost.

83. Define Your Vision & Commit to the Process
By: Coach Christopher Stack

Success in the college recruiting journey starts with a clear vision and unwavering commitment. Have you ever stopped, closed your eyes, and envisioned the type of college experience you want to pursue?

The "vision" step is about aligning your aspirations with what's realistic and attainable, while staying true to your passions and values – what you care about most.

Once your vision is clear, the next step is committing to the process.

This requires discipline, consistency, and a willingness to put in the time and effort. From creating a detailed plan with timelines and checklists, to engaging your support system of parents, coaches, and mentors, commitment is the key to staying focused and resilient through the ups and downs of recruiting.

When you define your vision and fully commit, you set the foundation for a successful and fulfilling recruiting journey.

How do you Define Your Vision?

- Identify your strengths, weaknesses, opportunities, and challenges.
- Unpack the motivations and driving forces behind your desire to compete at the next level. "Why do I want this?"
- Establish clear, actionable goals. (Follow the process in part 2 of this book!)
- Craft a personal mission statement that reflects your purpose and values.
- Create a vision statement to define your long-term aspirations.

How do you Commit to the Process?

- Commit to your Academics
- Commit to your Sport
- Commit to the Recruiting Work

Why it matters:

Without a clear vision and commitment, it's easy to feel lost. Defining your goals and staying dedicated will give you purpose and keep you moving forward, even when challenges arise.

Real Results

Sarah, a Class of 2026 standout high school soccer player, began her recruiting journey without a clear direction. Competing for a top-tier club team in Pennsylvania, she initially believed Division I was her only path.

However, through the process I laid out before, Sarah discovered her true passion was finding the perfect balance between her academic pursuits and athletic ambitions. She shifted her goal to playing for a top academic institution with a competitive Division III program.

By engaging in the Self-Discovery Process, Sarah gained valuable insight into her strengths and opportunities.

This clarity allowed her to create a compelling recruiting profile and focus her efforts on schools that aligned with her vision. Exciting stuff!

As a result, she has attracted significant interest from several highly respected Division III programs that excel in both academics and athletics.

84. Know the Landscape | By: Coach Christopher Stack

The college athlete landscape is getting more overwhelming and complex by the day; understanding it is vital to your successful navigation of the recruiting process.

Each athletic association (NCAA, NAIA, NJCAA) and division (I, II, III) offers unique opportunities, rules, and experiences, from competitive programs with athletic scholarships to schools prioritizing academics.

Familiarizing yourself with recruiting rules, timelines, and eligibility requirements helps you to stay on track and avoid missed opportunities.

How to Better Understand the Landscape:

- **Opportunities in College Sports:** College athletics comes in all shapes and sizes; a few are listed above. Take time to check out the different divisions, athletic associations, and scholarship opportunities available.
- **Rules and Guidelines:** There are rules that regulate recruiting for your sport. Research the key timelines, contact periods, and visit guidelines so you know what to expect.
- **Student-Athlete Experience:** Being a student-athlete looks different from school to school. Look beyond the sport and into the academics and campus culture.

Why it matters:

Understanding the landscape helps you make informed decisions and avoid surprises. The more you know, the better you can identify where you'll thrive both athletically and academically.

Real Story

Lucas, a Class of 2022 aspiring Division I lacrosse player, was initially unaware that there are only 78 men's Division I programs. After doing a deeper dive into the Men's Lacrosse Landscape, he discovered there were significantly more opportunities at the NCAA Division II and III levels.

This insight helped him recognize that while his Division I aspirations might have been unrealistic, there were excellent prospects to explore at Division II and III schools.

After building a list of potential programs and thoroughly researching their academics and athletics, Lucas had a solid understanding of his options. His proactive efforts paid off, leading him to an NCAA Division II school that perfectly aligned with his goals. His commitment to understanding the recruiting landscape and diligent preparation ultimately earned him a scholarship offer from a competitive Division II program that matched both his academic and athletic ambitions!

85. The Power of Academics | By: Coach Christopher Stack

I am going to be direct with you here: academics are king. If you are not dialed in on your studies, it's going to eventually cost you. Your academic performance typically determines your eligibility and scholarship opportunities, so you must take it seriously.

Maintaining strong grades and test scores not only meets NCAA, NAIA, or NJCAA eligibility requirements, but also opens doors to academic scholarships and programs that can reduce the financial burden of college. Who doesn't want that?!

A solid academic record shows coaches that you're disciplined and capable of balancing the demands of being a student-athlete. It shows that you are willing to put in the work on and off the field.

How to Prioritize Academics:

- **Eligibility Matters:** Ensure you meet the academic requirements for both the NCAA (or other associations) and your target schools. This includes maintaining a strong GPA and preparing for, and performing well on, standardized tests.

- **4-Year Academic Plan:** Work with your school counselor or career coach to create a plan that keeps you on track to meet eligibility standards. Include:
    - Graduation requirements
    - College prerequisites
    - Time for SAT/ACT prep

- **Balancing Sports and School:** Being a student-athlete in college will require excellent time management skills. Start building habits now to juggle academics, athletics, and extracurriculars successfully.

Why it matters:

Athletic ability can open doors, but academic focus and execution keeps them open. It may seem like your sport performance is the most important thing, but it becomes irrelevant if your academics are ignored.

Real Story

David, a Class of 2024 high school basketball player with NCAA Division II/III talent, initially underestimated the importance of academics in the recruiting process. When he reviewed his grades, he realized his opportunities would be limited unless he improved his academic performance. Fortunately, starting the process early gave him time to make meaningful changes.

With guidance from his counselors, David developed a plan to raise his GPA and become a stronger student. By his senior year, he not only met the eligibility requirements, but also secured a partial academic scholarship to a Division II school!

86. Research and Discover Your Best Fit | By: Coach Christopher Stack

Don't get lazy with this step. You may be the type of person who does not like doing research. Trust me, I get it! But remember this:

> *"The pain of discipline weighs ounces. The pain of regret weighs tons."*

Stick some glue on your seat, get in front of that computer, and research, research, research!

Finding the right college fit is about more than just athletics—it's about aligning your academic, athletic, social, and personal goals with the right program and environment.

Is the program a winning program? Is that important to you? What is the coaching style?

Does the college offer your major? What about other majors that you are semi-interested in as a back up?

What's the campus culture like? Does it match up with what you care about?

Where is this school? Does location matter?

This is your journey and it's a 4 year long one — spend meaningful time on this and choose the place that feels right for you!

Areas to Consider:

- ➤ Academics
- ➤ Campus Culture and Location
- ➤ Team Culture and Coach
- ➤ Financial Fit

Self-Reflection Activity:

Take time to write down what you need in college, both as a student and an athlete. In addition to the questions above, think about the following:

- ➤ What academic subjects or career paths interest you?
- ➤ What kind of coach and team dynamic would help you thrive?
- ➤ Do you want to stay close to home or explore new places?
- ➤ What does your ideal environment consist of?

Action Step: Visiting 5 or more colleges helps you get a true feel for the environment. Take note of the facilities, talk to current players, and sit in on a class if possible.

Real Story

Emily, a talented field hockey player in the Class of 2021, was receiving interest from schools at all levels. The overwhelming attention left her unsure of how to proceed. To gain clarity, Emily completed the "Discover Your Best Fit" activity, which helped her identify the most important factors she was seeking in her college experience.

After reassessing her priorities, she found a Division II school that offered her desired major, a supportive team culture, and a better overall fit for her personality. Although it was not convenient or easy, she was glad she took the time to make the best decision for her future!

87. Build Your Brand, Market Yourself, and Be Seen | By: Coach Christopher Stack

The world of college recruiting is competitive!

So how do you stand out? You have to "be in the room," build your personal brand, and follow up.

Being in the room is all about showing up to the places where you will get noticed.

Building your personal brand is showcasing the unique combination of your athletic skills, academic achievements, character, and values.

Following up is all about a relentless, professional pursuit of the schools you desire most.

Here are the 3 keys to building your brand and being seen:

1. Create a professional online presence.

This includes creating a good highlight reel on Hudl or Youtube, up-to-date stats, and a polished social media profile that reflects your goals and personality.

Don't post inappropriate content, ever. It will be seen!

2. Reach out to coaches with personalized emails

and show them why you're a great fit for their program.

Here is an example of a great email:

WINNING THE RECRUITING GAME

Subject Line: [Your Sport] Recruit: [Your Full Name], [Graduation Year] - [Your High School Name]

Dear Coach [Coach's Last Name],

*I hope you're doing well! My name is **[Your Full Name]**, and I am a **[Sport]** player at **[Your High School Name]** in **[City, State]**. I am reaching out to express my interest in **[College/University Name]** and your **[team/program]**. I have followed your program closely and am impressed by the culture you have created. I believe my skills and values align with what you are building at **[School Name]**. **[Insert any other personalized information you have noticed or appreciate about this school and program]**.*

*I am a **[position/role]** with **[number of years]** of experience in **[specific area of your sport]**, and I have a passion for **[briefly describe what excites you about your sport, the team, or the program]**. I understand at the collegiate level I may be called to a new position to best help the team– that's what teamwork is all about.*

*In my recent season, I achieved **[highlight notable achievements, stats, or accomplishments]**, and I am constantly working to improve both my athletic and academic performance.*

*Attached is my highlight reel, which showcases my recent performances. I would greatly appreciate the opportunity to discuss how I can contribute to your team. I am also including a link to my **Hudl/YouTube** profile for your convenience: **[insert link]**.*

*I am very excited about the possibility of joining your program and continuing to grow as an athlete at **[School Name]**. I would be honored to further discuss how I can fit into your recruiting class for **[year]**.*

Is there any additional information I can provide for you? Would you like to arrange a call or meeting?

Thank you for considering my email. I hope to hear from you soon.

Sincerely,

[Your Full Name]
[Your High School Name]
[Your Position/Role]
[Your Contact Information]
[Link to Hudl/YouTube/Profile]

EVERYTHING YOUNG ATHLETES SHOULD KNOW

3. Attend showcases, camps, and compete in the right tournaments.

Work with your coaches to find the right ones that match your recruiting goals. You do not need to attend one every single weekend, especially if you start early. The fewer options you have, the more you should attend.

Marketing yourself effectively is about telling your story in a way that sets you apart and demonstrates your commitment to success both on and off the field.

Why it matters:

When you are out of sight, you are out of mind. Coaches need to see what you bring to the table—your athletic talent, character, and potential. Taking charge of your marketing helps you control your narrative.

Lastly, make sure to track your progress. Use a spreadsheet to stay organized—track which coaches you've contacted, their responses, and any next steps.

Real Story

Elizabeth, a Class of 2025 high school soccer player for one of Maryland's top clubs, recognized that her work ethic and great attitude were her greatest strengths. With Division I aspirations and the talent to match, she began building her personal brand. She started sharing posts on Instagram showcasing her training sessions, team achievements, and volunteer work, tagging college programs of interest.

Her polished performances and authentic profile caught the attention of multiple schools, who admired her dedication and community involvement. To stand out even more, Elizabeth crafted a compelling "Elevator Pitch" and personally sent it to her target programs.

Coaches praised her creativity and unique approach. Her efforts paid off, earning her an athletic scholarship to a mid-major Division I school.

Elizabeth's journey highlights the power of a well-defined and genuine personal brand. By taking control of how she presented herself, she distinguished herself in a competitive recruiting landscape.

88. Weigh Your Options and Select the Best Fit

By: Coach Christopher Stack

While chapter 86 was about discovering your best fit, this chapter is where the rubber meets the road – selecting your college.

You are at the point where you crystallized your vision, committed to that vision, understand the landscape and what matters most to you, have built your brand and gained interest from colleges, and you have offers in hand.

Now it's time to evaluate each opportunity carefully and make a decision:

- ➤ **Evaluate Your Offers:** Once you've received interest or offers, take the time to compare them thoroughly. Look at the athletic, academic, and financial aspects of each option. **Ask yourself again:** Does this school align with my goals and values?
- ➤ **Trust Your Gut:** While data and logic are important, don't ignore how you feel. If a school feels like home and you're excited about the opportunity, it's likely the right fit.

Why it matters:

Your decision will shape the next four years of your life and beyond. Picking the best fit ensures that you'll be positioned to grow as a student, athlete, and individual. You can always change your mind and transfer, but that in itself is a challenging process. Do the work now and pick the best fit!

Real Story

Rachel, a high school softball player, received offers from several programs, eventually narrowing her options to a Division I and a Division III school. Although the Division I program promised greater visibility, Rachel valued a balance between academics and athletics. After visiting both campuses, speaking with coaches, current players and alumni, and seeking advice from mentors, Rachel chose the Division III school, which offered a 75% merit scholarship, strong academics, and a supportive team environment. This choice allowed her to thrive both on the field and in her studies, securing an internship in her chosen professional field!

89. College Sports: New Level, New Devil, New Skills Required

There is a saying that goes like this: *new level, new devil.* It's a bit odd, but it's actually a helpful saying for you to embrace as you get ready to transition from high-school to college.

College is different from high school athletics in so many ways, and not only in the ways most people think.

> "Practices are going to be harder. The competition is going to be better. I'm going to need to work harder."

Yes, of course. That's obvious.

But that's not all. You are going to need an entirely new set of skills if you are going to not only *survive*, but *thrive* in college sports your freshman year!

I worked with an athlete named Jess who went to college to play field hockey.

Everyone told her before going to college to have low expectations for playing time, that it was going to be overwhelming and stressful, and that she would "figure it out" by the end of freshman year.

I told her something that was the polar opposite. I told her that yes, it's a new level, and a new devil.

But I also asked her this question: *"Jess, what would it look like for you to start acting like a college athlete, with a college schedule, now? What would you do today to become better at time management? What can you do to raise your confidence levels today instead of waiting to get around that kind of competition?"*

Here is what she did:

1. She got a part-time job. This helped stretch her time management abilities like they would be stretched while playing college sports.
2. She looked for a new club team that was much more competitive, even though it would mean less playing time. This ensured that she would be ready for the elevated competition when she got to college.
3. She reached out to a friend of hers that was a freshman, already playing college field hockey, and asked her to send her over the *exact* types of workouts that she was doing to build her skills.

College sports will be a new level requiring higher skills in time management, work ethic, and productivity.

We know this, so let's start preparing now!

90. Behind the Recruiting Pitch: The Coach You Meet vs. The Coach You Get

After doing mindset coaching and personal training for hundreds of athletes who have gone on to play at the collegiate level, one thing I constantly hear is:

> *"The coach who recruited me and the coach I now play for are complete opposites. But they look the same!"*

The reality is that most coaches will do anything they can to get you to come to their school if they really want you.

I know *some* college coaches who are the same person through and through, but that is unfortunately not the norm.

In this book, I simply want to make you aware, to "warn you," that the coach you meet may not be the coach you play for.

Is there anything you can do to avoid going to a school where the coach is horribly mean and awful even though they seemed great during the recruiting phase? Yes!

Here are a few suggestions:

1. **During your recruiting trip, ask the current players what the coach is really like.** Have the courage to ask them if the coach was different during the recruiting phase. You aren't trying to get them to sell the coach out, you just want to know what to expect and what you are getting yourself into. It's worth it.
2. **During the trip, ask about athletes who have left the program.** Ask, "What made them leave?"

3. **Get better at interviewing.** Here are 5 great questions to ask the coach during the recruiting phase:

   a) What is your coaching philosophy and approach to player development?

   b) What are the best parts about the current team culture and what are the challenges?

   c) What do you look for in your players, both in and out of sports, and how do you determine who gets playing time?

   d) How do you balance athletics with academics, and what support systems are in place for student-athletes time management and mental health?

   e) What happens if a player decides to transfer or leave the program early? What is your approach to handling that situation?

At the end of the day, whether the coach is amazing or not, you can always learn from difficult situations. The coach will not be the reason you succeed or fail. How you choose to react and respond, will!

91. Pause: Is Playing College Sports REALLY What You Want?

A mistake many young athletes make is deciding early on that they are *going* to play college sports no matter what.

Year after year they take steps toward this dream, getting further married to the identity and decision that they once made in their younger years.

Their passions and desires change overtime and as they get to their sophomore or junior year, they feel like they "have to" continue pursuing their dream of playing college sports.

EVERYTHING YOUNG ATHLETES SHOULD KNOW

"I've been preparing my whole life for this. If I don't do it, I feel like I wasted all that time and money. People will be disappointed in me."

This is not a healthy way to think. There is actually a psychological term for this called the *Sunk Cost Fallacy.*

Sunk Cost Fallacy:

Imagine you've been watching a TV show for several seasons, and at first, you really enjoyed it. But by the latest season, the plot is getting boring, the characters are annoying, and you're just not interested anymore. But instead of stopping, you keep watching episode after episode because you've already invested so much time into the show. You think, "I've watched this much, I can't stop now. I've come too far to quit."

That's the sunk cost fallacy.

It's when you keep doing something just because you've already invested a lot of time or energy, even if it's not helping you get where you want to go. It's like staying in a bad situation just because you don't want to "waste" everything you've put in, even though stopping might be the best choice for your future.

Sometimes, it's better to step back and make a choice based on what's best for you *now*—not just because of what you've already done.

College sports require a huge amount of effort just to get the opportunity to get on a roster. They require 10x more effort when you actually *get there*.

At the same time, they will push you, challenge you, and be incredibly rewarding. They will set you up for future success in life.

Just make sure you really, really want to do it. It's a commitment, not a hobby.

A comforting truth that should reduce some of your anxiety about this decision is that *most* decisions are reversible.

Even if you decide to play freshman year, you can always decide otherwise after your first year. Again, don't let Sunk Cost Fallacy paralyze your decision making abilities!

THE NINTH
ESSENTIAL AREA OF MASTERY

EMPOWERING FEMALE ATHLETES:

OPTIMIZING PERFORMANCE WITHOUT SACRIFICING HEALTH

92. 6 Unique Needs for Female Athletes

Why include a section specifically for female athletes?

Because young female athletes need better quality, more memorable, more actionable education if they are going to thrive in and out of sports.

Unfortunately, while most of the information out there for athlete performance is not *specifically* targeted toward males, it does not do a good job at considering the unique design of the female athlete.

Here are the 6 primary things you need to know and do if you are a young female athlete who wants to perform at your highest level:

- ➢ How hormones and menstrual cycles affect performance
- ➢ The female athlete triad, bone health, and preventing injury
- ➢ How to strength train for peak athletic development
- ➢ How to prevent preventable ACL injuries
- ➢ Mindset and body image: How to be resilient and unshakeable
- ➢ Important nutrition considerations for the female athlete

In this section I am bringing in a leading expert in female athlete training, Justin Kegley.

Justin is a good friend of mine and author of books like "Be Great Today" and "High-Performance Nutrition for High School Athletes: A Guide for Athletes and Parents to Fuel for Maximum Performance."

He is the subject matter expert on this topic and I am expecting you will take away many valuable insights from his contributions.

93. Performance Training for the Female Athlete | By: Justin Kegley

Erin wasn't supposed to "make it." She's 5'5", which was too short to be a goalkeeper. She couldn't kick the ball far enough, wasn't fast enough, and tore her ACL as a freshman in high school.

But she had a clearly defined goal.

A D1 soccer scholarship.

I met Erin 10 years ago when she walked into Movement Fitness, my new training facility in Rockford, IL, looking to return to the field following her ACL tear.

She wasn't precisely the athlete that I wanted to train.

I wanted to train football and baseball players because that's who I was, who I had trained before, and who I was comfortable with.

When she came in, I had never trained a female athlete, a soccer player, or anyone that had torn their ACL.

I took what I knew and then studied like crazy to figure out how we could help her progress back, building speed, power, and strength, while also working to ensure we did everything we could to avoid another injury.

It was trial and error, but she continued to make progress over time.

We grew together.

Over the next few years, she continued to train 3-5 days per week, building the physical and mental capabilities to earn her a scholarship.

That offer she'd been hoping for finally came.

Her persistence and effort ultimately led her to earn Big Ten All-Conference Honors and the opportunity to play in the NWSL!

Training female athletes has become my passion and purpose. Over the last 10 years, I have trained thousands of female athletes to maximize their performance, minimize their injury risk, and build unshakeable confidence.

My goal is to give you the keys to do the same for yourself to ultimately become who you were created to be.

94. 3 Steps to Prevent ACL Injuries, Part 1 | By: Justin Kegley

You've seen it.

During a game a girl makes a sudden move, likely with no one around her; she screams and then falls to the ground, clutching her knee.

Maybe you were that girl.

It's awful.

Female athletes between the ages of 14-18 are up to 8 times more likely to tear their ACLs than male athletes of the same age.

Approximately 32,000 high school female athletes will tear their ACL this year—22,000 more in college.

I hate these numbers.

I don't tell you these statistics to make you afraid to play; I tell you so that you are aware and work to create a solution that will keep you from being one of them.

I can't guarantee it won't happen, but there's good news. At least 70% of injuries can be reduced through proper training!

That training can not only reduce your risk of injury, but also lead to incredible increases in speed, power, strength, and overall performance.

If you want to play at a higher level and develop the confidence to reach your full potential, all while reducing the chances of an injury, you need to be strong and powerful. Start by training year-round, both in-season & off-season. The difficulty and amount of training will vary, but training consistently will make a significant difference in your performance, injury reduction, and your confidence.

Once you have established a year-round training schedule, it's time to focus on how you are training. There are 3 key steps to effective performance training for the female athlete:

1. Move well first
2. Progressive plyometrics (especially single leg)
3. Strength training (especially single leg)

Step 1: Move Well First

The first step is to make sure you can move in a way that will allow you to play your sports effectively.

The good news is that this isn't a long process! It's a matter of consistently putting in the daily work.

Essentially, it's a thorough warm-up.

Warm-ups are easy to do, but also easy to skip because they don't seem like they are doing much.

EVERYTHING YOUNG ATHLETES SHOULD KNOW

The long-term effect of taking a few minutes before and after your practices, training, and games can have a massive impact on your body's overall health.

The truth is that if you can't take this seriously, you aren't ready to be your best.

One of my coaches, Brian Cain, has a saying: "Do a little, a lot."

Do a little bit of work, often.

This phrase is simple but effective in sports, school, and life.

When it comes to caring for your body, moving through a series of drills and exercises before you start playing can make a significant difference.

It will help you improve or maintain your mobility and prevent tightness in your hips, lower back, knees, and shoulders.

Your seasons are long, and though you may not feel it now, they *will* take a toll on your body. Consistently and effectively warming up will pay off big time in the long run.

Here is a simple warm-up you can do to help you improve your joint health and flexibility.

1. Couch Stretch (:60 per side)
2. Calf Stretch (:60 per leg)
3. World's Greatest Stretch (2x per side)
4. Split Squats (8 x per leg)
5. Lateral Squats (8 x per leg)
6. Single Leg Deadlift (8 x per leg)

7. Pogo Hops (:30 x 2)
8. Carioca (5 rotations per leg)
9. March and Skipping (5 Marches and 5 Skips per leg)

These movements require no equipment and very little space. Yes, there are more things you can do, but as a baseline, before and after, these movements can help you to consistently move well.

Step 2: Progressive Plyometrics

Step two is performing progressive plyometrics, which is essentially a step-by-step approach to helping you jump better.

Honestly, this should be incorporated in every workout or warm up in one way or another.

There are many ways to do this well; the important thing is that it needs to be done.

In season, out of season - it doesn't matter. Incorporating progressive plyometrics is one of the primary keys to reducing injury risk.

The very first thing that is required for plyometrics is to land well!

Did you know that 70% of ACL tears happen without contact? This means no one was around you, no one pushed you, and no one touched your knee.

There are three main culprits non-contact ACL tears:

1. Poor landing mechanics
    - Stiff Legged Landing
    - Valgus Knee Landing
    - Landing with your body outside the center of mass

EVERYTHING YOUNG ATHLETES SHOULD KNOW

2. Poor deceleration, or the inability to stop
3. Poor change of direction ability

First, we have to ensure that you can control your body. Let's start by making sure you can land correctly on two legs.

When you land from a vertical jump, make sure you land with your feet under your shoulders, with your hips, knees, and ankles in a straight line, while maintaining great posture in the upper body.

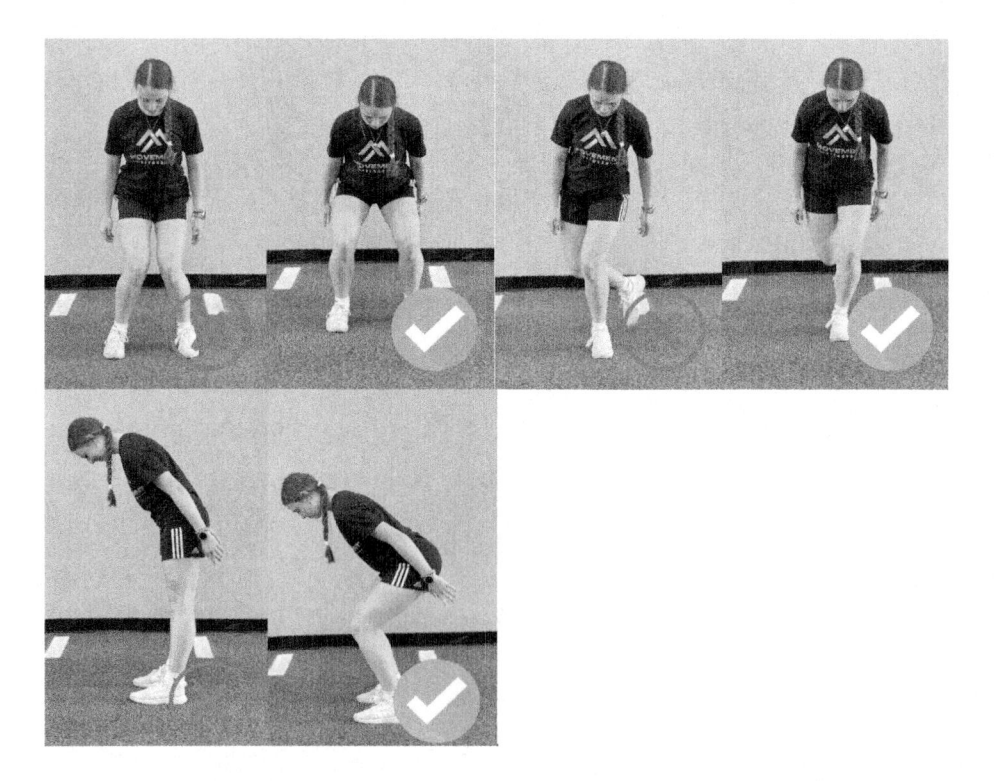

Work to absorb the ground, not landing stiffly, while ensuring your knees never come together.

You must learn to align your knees with your hips. The angle of the hip to the knee for female athletes makes this more difficult naturally, so you will have to work on this.

Landing hard puts a lot of wear and tear on your joints, so the sooner you master these tips, the better.

Practice on your own so you know you're landing safely in practice and games. You can do this by jumping onto a box, vertical jumping in place, or landing after stepping off a box. Practice this until you can consistently and repeatedly land safely.

Once you can land on two feet well, you can start progressing the pace of the jumps. If you are confident in your ability to stick the jump, advance to a mini-bounce followed by repeat jumps. This can be done with hurdles or without - you decide what works best for you!

Next, you can progress to jumping and landing on one leg. The rules for landing on one leg are the same as landing on two legs, it's just more difficult. Challenge yourself!

There are many ways to perform plyometrics; you can find more ideas and examples at **www.completefemaleathlete.com**.

Performing plyometrics safely requires high levels of coordination, stability, and strength; it's not going to happen on the first try. But when you put in the work, you'll take your training to the next level - while staying injury free!

95. 3 Steps to Prevent ACL Injuries, Part 2 | By: Justin Kegley

Step 3: Strength Training

Ava was an athlete I worked with who earned a scholarship to play volleyball at a DII school in Wisconsin. The first day she reported to camp, they tested each player's strength and conditioning.

As they went to the chin-up bar, not one player could do a single chin-up.

Except Ava.

She did 12 continuous chin-ups. Talk about a confidence boost!

In that moment she was able to stand out and make an impact on her new coaches and teammates.

Being strong is not something that can be given to you. It is only achieved by putting in consistent effort and continually challenging yourself.

Fundamentally, working to master push-ups and chin-ups is a must. Female athletes gain a new level of confidence when they can do those two things.

Similar to plyometrics, the goal is to start by mastering foundational movements.

Your core is essential because all force is transmitted through it. If you don't have a stable core, you won't be able to jump, sprint, cut, hit, throw, kick, or perform any movement with a high degree of success.

Single leg strength is another essential area for female athletes to master. Split squats, single leg squats, single leg deadlifts, and lateral squats are examples of exercises that help with single leg strength development.

Single-leg training allows us to do two things: reduce injury risk and enhance performance.

First, it allows us to reduce injury risk by assessing imbalances. If one side is stronger than the other, that leads to inefficient movement patterns which can impact performance and increase injury risk.

Your legs should be really close in terms of strength. If one leg is significantly stronger than the other, that is a problem.

Second, single-leg training enhances our athletic performance by increasing power and agility.

Most sports are played on one leg at a time. Being able to jump, cut, and sprint requires a fundamental strength from each of your legs individually.

Between your warmup, plyometrics, and strength training, you should spend a significant amount of training time on one leg!

96. Nutrition for the Female Athlete, Part 1 | By: Justin Kegley

To perform at your highest level, you must eat like an elite athlete.

Nutrition for female athletes can be challenging because it's not just about fueling for performance; societal pressures about body image also play a huge role.

Myths, like protein making you bulky or carbs and fats leading to weight gain, persist, and everyone's unique body structure and metabolism make nutrition even more complex.

Eating to fuel performance is different from eating to look "skinny." Playing sports requires a lot of energy, and the right foods help with recovery after intense training. Unfortunately, many female athletes don't eat enough. There are many reasons for this:

1. Lacking knowledge about what to eat and when
2. Unintentional undereating
3. Not planning your meals in advance

4. Eating a restrictive diet for physical appearance or weight loss
5. Suffering from eating disorders

Before we go any further, remember this: your worth is not defined by what the world says about you. My personal belief is that you are fearfully and wonderfully made by a God who loves you and designed you in a perfect way.

Your body has specific features—some you can change and others you can't. Don't harm your body to please others. It takes time and planning to build good habits. Preparing meals, creating grocery lists, and eating consistently don't happen accidentally. But the time and energy you put into your nutrition are well worth it!

You can't skip breakfast and expect to have enough energy for the day. Lunch has to be more than just whatever is served in the cafeteria. And eating before and after a practice or game is essential for energy maintenance and recovery.

Almost every athlete burns more calories than they consume, which can lead to a condition called the Female Athlete Triad, which consists of:

1. Low energy availability
2. Menstrual disturbances
3. Low bone mineral density

Let's dive into each category so you avoid these common mistakes.

1. Low Energy Availability

Low energy availability occurs when you don't eat enough to match the calories you burn, leading to sluggishness, fatigue, and an inability to give your best effort during practice.

But despite feeling tired, many athletes push themselves harder by training more. This is a recipe for poor focus in school, slower recovery from minor injuries.

"No problem, Coach! I'll grab an energy drink!"

No! Caffeine as a primary response is a crutch that creates sleep disturbances, rapid heart rate, stomach issues, as well as increases the risk of anxiety and nervousness.

For teenage female athletes, nutritional guidelines suggest a daily intake of 2200-2600 calories, with about 15-20% of those calories from protein. This is significantly more food than many athletes consume, and it's often more protein than most are used to. If you need help, consider consulting a sports nutritionist for more personalized guidance.

2. *Menstrual Disturbances*

Low energy intake can also lead to menstrual disturbances. Your body needs adequate energy to maintain hormone balance and regular periods. If energy levels dip too low, periods may become irregular or stop altogether. This disruption can impact your bone health, as it affects a hormone called estradiol, which keeps bones strong.

I know, this is a lot of new information and some big words. You don't have to memorize it all; the key is that you are now paying attention.

3. *Low Bone Mineral Density*

Back to estradiol. Without enough of it, your bones may become weak and lose density, increasing your risk of fractures and osteoporosis down the road.

To combat the Female Athlete Triad, you must learn how to fuel your body properly. Eating enough, balancing your nutrients, and prioritizing

EVERYTHING YOUNG ATHLETES SHOULD KNOW

recovery will help you thrive both on and off the field. The next chapter will give you examples of what to eat and when to eat it!

97. Nutrition for the Female Athlete, Part 2 | By: Justin Kegley

To combat the Female Athlete Triad and maximize performance, you must learn how to fuel your body properly. Not sure where to start? With your first meal of the day, of course!

Start with Breakfast

Unfortunately, breakfast is not a priority for many teenagers. I'm sure you have a "good" reason for skipping breakfast:

- You don't wake up on time.
- You struggle to get moving in the morning.
- You aren't hungry.
- You don't plan, so you don't know what to eat.

Any of those sound familiar? I've been guilty of a few, too. But that was before I understood the importance of my first meal each day. Prioritizing breakfast is a non-negotiable.

But what should breakfast include?

- **Protein:** to help build and repair your muscles
- **Fat:** to support brain and joint function and provide long-term energy
- **Carbs:** these are the body's primary energy source, particularly for fueling tough practices and games

At the end of this section I'll give you access to exactly what an athlete should eat for breakfast, lunch, pre-workout, post-workout, and dinner. Keep reading!

Next up: Lunch!

Lunch is essential, especially when you have practice or a game later in the day. It should also include all three macronutrients—protein, fats, and carbohydrates. Since cafeteria food is not typically known for being the most nutritious, packing your lunch is often the best option. Include macros that will fuel you for the rest of the day; and remember to pick foods you look forward to eating!

Eating Before and After Workouts

To perform your best, nutrition before and after workouts is critical. Workouts include practices, games, or any moderate to high-intensity training.

Pre-Workout Nutrition: Eat a snack that includes protein (10-20g) and carbohydrates (30-60g) about 30-60 minutes before your workout. This will help regulate blood sugar and fuel your performance.

Post-Workout Nutrition: After a workout, you should eat within 30 minutes to kickstart recovery. The focus should be on carbohydrates and protein with limited fats, because fats slow digestion. Aim for a 2:1 or 3:1 carbohydrate-to-protein ratio. You should consume about 40-75g of carbohydrates and 20-25g of protein.

Finish Strong with Dinner

When possible, aim to eat home-cooked meals. Preparing meals at home gives you control over the ingredients and ensures balanced nutrition. If

EVERYTHING YOUNG ATHLETES SHOULD KNOW

you're eating out, choose options wisely to avoid unhealthy choices from fast food.

Eating well requires planning. Yes, you are going to have to go talk to mom and dad, admit they were right all along about this, and ask to go grocery shopping with them. Hopefully that conversation is quick and painless!

Nutrition is a major X-factor for performance and health that rarely gets enough energy and attention. It's time to zero in on this major area and begin treating your nutrition game with the same focus that you do your skills and athletic abilities!

Athlete Performance Bonus Bundle: As promised, I want to give you access to a detailed plan that tells you exactly what to eat throughout your day. No more guesswork. It's free for you as a thank you for reading this book. Head to **www.andrewjsimpson.com/everything-bonus** to get the "What to Eat and When to Eat It" bonus for athletes.

THE TENTH
ESSENTIAL AREA OF MASTERY

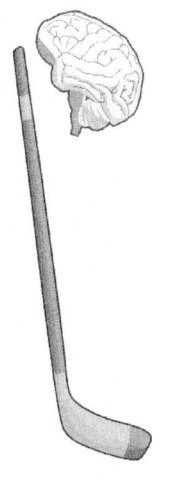

INSPIRING GREATNESS:

10 LITTLE KNOWN TIPS FOR ATHLETES WITH TRANSFORMATIONAL POWER

98. Luck vs. Hard work

> *"Hard work puts you where good luck can find you."*
> -PAT RILEY, NBA Coach

Said another way, luck is when preparation meets opportunity.

Along your journey to reaching your dreams of being an all-conference player, standing on a college field, or perhaps even making it pro, you will need a combination of both hard work *and* luck.

How do you get lucky? Work hard and work smart every day, every week, every month, every season, and every year.

Good luck tends to find those who work the hardest over the longest period of time!

99. Keep Going Until You Get it Right

> *"Champions keep playing until they get it right."*
> -BILLIE JEAN KING, Tennis Icon

Checking the box is not the same as doing something with excellence. Coach John Wooden once said, "Make each day your masterpiece."

Whether you are practicing a skill, tying your shoes, cleaning your room, stringing your stick, or lying in your bed and shooting a basketball toward the ceiling, do it to the absolute best of your ability.

If you have a certain skill you are working to per-fect, keep working at it until you get it right.

Oftentimes, the breakthrough is right on the other side of the biggest point of frustration when you most want to give up!

100. Practice Like It's Gametime

> *"The more you sweat in practice, the less you bleed in battle."*
> -RICHARD MARCINKO, Former Navy SEAL (often quoted by Tim Tebow, former pro football player)

Remember this one next time you go to practice. Don't take it easy at practice. Take it up 3 notches.

Play at practice like it's the final 2 minutes of a championship game.

You will never play the way you practice. You will always play one notch below.

Therefore, bring your A++ game to every practice, every day. Because the more you sweat at practice, the less you "bleed" in games!

Rate Your Practice Intensity and Focus Scale of 1-10: _____

Based on your goals, where should it be? _____/10

What decision will you make starting today to practice like it's gametime?

_____

_____

_____

_____

101. It's You vs. You

> *"You don't play against opponents. You play against the game of basketball."*
>
> — **BOBBY KNIGHT,** College Basketball Coach

Some athletes get so focused on the desire to be better than everyone else, an uncontrollable aspect of any sport, that they fail to focus on being better than they were yesterday.

Coach Bobby Knight takes it to another level with this quote. "The game of basketball" is referring to understanding and executing the fundamentals—strategy, technique, discipline, teamwork, etc., of any sport you play.

What are the fundamentals in your sport? What do the best athletes in your sport focus on constantly improving?

In the space below, write about the fundamentals of your sport and how you plan to master them!

_____
_____
_____
_____
_____
_____

102. Willpower Doesn't Work

> *"It's not the will to win that matters—everyone has that. It's the will to prepare to win that matters."*
> -PAUL "BEAR" BRYANT, College Football Coach

If you are going to become the best you can be, you must prepare for it. But eventually, your willpower will run out. Remember earlier in the section on goal setting when we talked about Why-power > Will-power?

You must, must, must tap back into your "Why," the reason you are doing this to begin with. In fact, since I really want to see you have the WILL to prepare to win, go ahead and re-write your BHAG (Big Goal) and your "Why" for wanting to achieve it, below.

Don't skip this. If you are serious about your dreams, you will do this exercise again and again and again!

MY BHAG:

_____

_____

_____

_____

MY WHY:

_____

_____

_____

_____

103. Don't Just Go Through The Motions

> *"I don't count the days. I make the days count."*
>
> - **MUHAMMAD ALI,** Boxing Legend

It's not about doing more. *More* isn't always *better*. More strength training done with bad form = decreased results. More running without strategic sprint interval training won't result in you actually getting faster.

Muhammed Ali knew something many athletes don't, and that's why he became the greatest to ever play the game. He knew that it wasn't about the hours he put in, but what he put into the hours.

Let me say that again. It's not the hours you put into practice that matter, *it's about what you put into the hours* that matters most!

104. Sports are a Gift, not an Entitlement

> *"When you have the ability to do something, you have a responsibility to do it."*
>
> - **LEBRON JAMES,** NBA basketball superstar

How do you define greatness? Being dominant? Crushing your opponents?

I define greatness as someone who does the best they can to become the best they can be, while inspiring and helping as many others as they possibly can along the way.

Do you think more highly of a player who was only in it for themselves? Or, the player who was always looking to use their gifts, talents, and influence others to also shine brightly?

Most of us would say the second one, of course!

When you have the ability to play the game you love and become great at it, you have a responsibility to do it. When you have the ability to encourage, inspire, or mentor another younger athlete to become better, you have the responsibility to do it.

As Uncle Ben famously said to his nephew Peter Parker (also known as Spiderman),

> "With great power comes great responsibility."

105. Vulnerability is Power

> "There is a crack in everything, that's how the light gets in."
> -ELIZABETH GILBERT, Author of Eat, Pray, Love

Mental health precedes peak physical performance. If you want to play the game you love long enough, and at a high level, you must prioritize mental health.

One of the ways to do this is to be vulnerable.

Everyone knows you have flaws, because everyone knows they have flaws.

So, since everyone already knows that you have flaws, you might as well receive a benefit from that and admit it openly.

When you are struggling, tell someone. When life feels heavy, remove the load by talking to someone. When you do this, you free yourself and you also give another person the opportunity to help you.

Remember, vulnerability is not weakness. Vulnerability is power.

106. The Secret to Never Ending Motivation

> *"You are never too old to set another goal or to dream a new dream."*
>
> -C.S. LEWIS (often quoted by Tom Brady, NFL Quarterback)

I worked with a college athlete named Carly who became an absolute beast while playing college basketball. She ended up achieving way more than she ever intended to while she was in college.

After she graduated, about 6 months went by and I received this message from her– *"Coach Andrew, I am struggling to find motivation. I am working now and it's just not the same as playing for a team like I did in college. How do I get motivated? This is so hard."*

I had failed Carly. I did not set her up for success after sports and that's why I am writing this to you here, now.

The secret to staying motivated is to *keep finding new things to challenge you and setting goals to work toward.*

After that conversation, she did a few things:

1. She found a fitness challenge with a community.

She began going to this gym to work on this particular challenge 3 days a week, with other people who were also working toward the same challenge.

2. She created 30-day challenges.

- ➤ 30-day "no complaining" challenge to help her take more ownership
- ➤ 30-day "no social media" challenge to help her ease some anxiety and take back control of her mind

- 30-day "power of one" challenge where she would call or message a new person everyday just to encourage them and let them know she was thinking about them
- 30-day "chapter a day" challenge where she would read one chapter of the Bible everyday to grow closer to God
- 30-day "no caffeine" challenge where she would reset her adrenal system and prove to herself that she did not need to rely on artificial energy drinks for focus and productivity

The secret to motivation is the three C's: Challenge, Community, and Consistency.

107. Choose Fun, Play the Long Game

We are finishing out this book with the number one, most important thing about sports.

> "I want to have fun. I want to make it a fun experience, win or lose, I'm going to have fun."
> - SHAQUILLE O'NEAL, NBA HALL OF FAMER

> "I love what I do, and I just try to have fun with it."
> - SIMONE BILES, USA GYMNASTICS OLYMPIC CHAMPION

> "I'm not doing this for any other reason other than I love the sport and I have fun doing it."
> - MICHAEL PHELPS, USA SWIMMING OLYMPIC CHAMPION

"But coach Andrew, I have huge goals. I want to be the best. And that requires WORK, not just fun."

If you are truly playing the long game, you know that fun is an essential ingredient.

If you do not have fun doing what you are doing, at some point, you are not going to perform to the best of your ability.

I've talked with thousands of athletes and they all say the same thing: "I play my best when I am having fun."

Choose fun. When it's hard, choose fun. When you are tired, choose fun.

Gamify practices and skill work with your friends. Create challenges and contests. Do whatever you need to do to make it fun, because fun leads to future success.

CONCLUSION

There you have it. Over 101 essential skills, strategies, and pro tips for thriving in sports.

Read one everyday.

Every 3 months, you will get through the entire book.

That means you can read this book almost 4 times each year by reading just one chapter a day!

Things do not change in a day, they change *daily*. A little effort overtime compounds to create extraordinary results.

Now go out there, choose joy, build others up, and be the best you can be today!

GET COACH ANDREW'S ENTIRE ATHLETE SUCCESS BOOK SERIES

The Unstoppable Athlete: 12 Keys to Unlock Your Full Potential [The Only One Who Can Stop You, Is You]

The Youth Truth: a proven playbook for coaches and parents to develop confident, healthy, wildly successful athletes without adding pressure or pushing them away from sports

Athlete! 7 Mindset Hacks to Dominate in Sports and Life: proven strategies for teen and college athletes to stop overthinking, get out of their head, and finally master their mental health and mindset

Printed in Great Britain
by Amazon